TOGAF Version 8.1.1 Enterprise Edition
Study Guide

GW00889115

Other publications by Van Haren Publishing

Van Haren Publishing (VHP) specializes in titles on Best Practices, methods and standards within IT management. Architecture (Enterprise and IT, business management and project management.

These publications are grouped in the series, eg: *ITSM Library* (on behalf of ITSMF International), *Best Practice* and *IT Management Topics*. VHP is also publisher on behalf of leading companies and institutions, eg The Open Group, IPMA-NL, CA, Getronics, Pink Elephant). At the time of going to press the following books are available:

IT (Service) Management / IT Governance
ITSM, ITIL® V3 and ITIL® V2
Foundations of IT Service Management – based on ITIL® V3
  (English, Dutch, German; French, Japanese and Spanish
  editions: Spring 2008)
Introduction to IT Service Management (ITIL V3, English)
IT Service Management based on ITIL V3 – A Pocket Guide
  (English, Dutch, German, Italian; French, Japanese and
  Spanish editions: Spring 2008)
Foundations of IT Service Management based on ITIL® (ITIL V2),
  (English, Dutch, French, German, Spanish, Japanese, Chinese,
  Danish, Italian, Korean, Russian, Arabic; also available as a
  CD-ROM)
Implementing Service and Support Management Processes (English)
*Release and Control for IT Service Management, based on ITIL® - A
  Practitioner Guide* (English)

ISO/IEC 20000
ISO/IEC 20000 – An Introduction
  (English, German: Spring 2008)
Implementing ISO/IEC 20000 Certification (English: Spring 2008)
ISO/IEC 20000 - A Pocket Guide (English, Italian, German,
  Spanish, Portuguese)

ISO 27001 and ISO 17799
*Information Security based on ISO 27001 and ISO 17799 -
  A Management Guide* (English)
*Implementing Information Security based on ISO 27001 and ISO
  17799 - A Management Guide* (English)

CobiT
IT Governance based on CobiT4.1® - A Management Guide
  (English, German)

IT Service CMM
IT Service CMM - A Pocket Guide (English)

ASL and BiSL
ASL - A Framework for Application Management
  (English, German)
ASL - Application Services Library - A Management Guide
  (English, Dutch)
BiSL - A Framework for Business Information Management
  (Dutch, English)
BiSL - Business information Services Library - A Management Guide
  (Dutch; English)

ISPL
IT Services Procurement op basis van ISPL (Dutch)
IT Services Procurement based on ISPL – A Pocket Guide (English)

Other IT Management titles:
De RfP voor IT-outsourcing
  (Dutch; English version due Spring 2008)
Decision- en Controlfactoren voor IT-Sourcing (Dutch)
Defining IT Success through the Service Catalogue (English)
Frameworks for IT Management - An introduction (English,
  Japanese; Dutch)
Frameworks for IT Management – A Pocket Guide
  (English, German, Dutch)
Implementing IT Governance (English)
Implementing leading standards for IT management
  (English, Dutch)
IT Service Management global best practices, volume (English)
IT Service Management Best Practices, volumes 1, 2, 3 and 4
  (Dutch)

ITSM from hell! / ITSM from hell based on Not ITIL (English)
ITSMP - The IT Strategy Management Process (English)
Metrics for IT Service Management (English, Russian)
Service Management Process Maps (English)
Six Sigma for IT Management (English)
Six Sigma for IT Management – A Pocket Guide (English)

MOF/MSF
MOF - Microsoft Operations Framework, A Pocket Guide
  (Dutch, English, French, German, Japanese)
MSF - Microsoft Solutions Framework, A Pocket Guide
  (English, German)

Architecture (Enterprise and IT)
*TOGAF, The Open Group Architecture Framework – A
  Management Guide* (English)
The Open Group Architecture Framework – 2007 Edition
  (English, official publication of TOG)
TOGAF™ Version 8 Enterprise Edition – Study Guide
  (English, official publication of TOG)
TOGAF™ Version 8.1.1 Enterprise Edition –A Pocket Guide
  (English, official publication of TOG)

Business Management
ISO 9000
ISO 9001:2000 - The Quality Management Process (English)

EFQM
*The EFQM excellence model for Assessing Organizational
  Performance – A Management Guide* (English)

SqEME®
Process management based on SqEME® (English)
SqEME® – A Pocket Guide (English, Dutch, mid 2008)

Project/Programme/Risk Management
ICB/NCB
NCB Versie 3– Nederlandse Competence Baseline
  (Dutch, on behalf of IPMA-NL)
Projectmanagement op basis van NCB V3 - IPMA-C en IPMA-D
  (Dutch)

PRINCE2™
Project Management based on PRINCE2™- Edition 2005
  (English, Dutch, German)
PRINCE2™ - A No Nonsense Management Guide (English)
PRINCE2™ voor opdrachtgevers – Management Guide (Dutch)

MINCE®
MINCE® – A Framework for Organizational Maturity (English)

MSP
Programme Management based on MSP (English, Dutch)
Programme Management based on MSP - A Management Guide
  (English)

M_o_R
Risk Management based on M_o_R - A Management Guide
  (English)

Other publications on project management:
Wegwijzer voor methoden bij Projectvolwassenheid
  (Dutch: fall 2008)
Het Project Management Office – Management Guide (Dutch)

For the latest information on VHP publications, visit our website:
www.vanharen.net

TOGAF™ Version 8.1.1 Enterprise Edition
Study Guide

Prepared by
Rachel Harrison

THE *Open* GROUP
www.opengroup.org

Van Haren
PUBLISHING

Colofon

Title:	TOGAF™ Version 8.1.1 Enterprise Edition – Study Guide
A Publication of:	The Open Group
Author:	prof. Rachel Harrison
Publisher:	Van Haren Publishing, Zaltbommel, www.vanharen.net
ISBN(13)	978 90 8753 093 8
Edition:	Second edition, first impression, October 2007
	Second edition, second impression, May 2008
Layout and Cover design:	CO2 Premedia, Amersfoort-NL
Print:	Wilco, Amersfoort-NL
Copyright:	2006, 2007 The Open Group

The views expressed in this Study Guide are not necessarily those of any particular member of The Open Group.
In the event of any discrepancy between text in this Study Guide and the official TOGAF 8.1.1 documentation, the TOGAF 8.1.1 documentation remains the authoritative version for certification, testing by examination, and other purposes. The official TOGAF 8.1.1 documentation can be obtained via Van Haren Publishing and via The Open Group.

Any comments relating to the material contained in this document may be submitted by email to: OGSpecs@opengroup.org.

For any further enquiries about Van Haren Publishing, please send an email to: info@vanharen.net.

Trademarks

Contents

Part 3 TOGAF Foundation Architecture

Part 6   Architecture Governance

Preface

This Document
This document is a Study Guide for TOGAF™ Version 8.1.1 Enterprise
Edition.

It gives an overview of every learning objective for the TOGAF 8 Certified
Course Syllabus and in-depth coverage on preparing and taking the TOGAF
8 Certified Examination. It is specifically designed to help professional
architects prepare for TOGAF 8 certification.

The audience for this Study Guide is:
• IT architects considering or planning to use TOGAF 8.1.1 Enterprise
Edition in their IT architecture projects
• Senior managers who need an understanding of TOGAF 8.1.1 Enterprise
Edition
• All those wishing to become TOGAF 8 Certified

A prior knowledge of IT architecture is advantageous but not required.
While reading this Study Guide, the reader should also refer to the
TOGAF 8 Enterprise Edition documentation[1] available online at
www.opengroup.org/architecture/togaf8-doc/arch and also available as
TOGAF "The Book".

The Study Guide is structured as shown below. The order of topics
corresponds to the six parts of the TOGAF 8 Certified Course Syllabus (see
Appendix D).
• Chapter 1 (Introduction), provides a brief introduction to TOGAF
certification and the TOGAF 8 Certified Examination, as well as how to
use this Study Guide.
• Part 1: TOGAF 8.1.1 Architecture Development Method (ADM)
 – Process, consists of Chapters 2 through 14:
  — Chapter 2 provides a high-level view of TOGAF, enterprise
   architecture, architecture frameworks, and the contents of TOGAF.
  — Chapter 3 provides an introduction to the Architecture Development
   Method (ADM), the method that TOGAF provides to develop IT

[1] TOGAF™ Version 8.1.1, 2007 Edition, ISBN 978 90 8753 094 5, Van Haren Publshing, www.vanharen.net

enterprise architectures. It also describes the ADM Architecture Requirements Management, a process that applies throughout the ADM. Subsequent chapters describe each phase of the Architecture Development Method (ADM) process.

— Chapter 4 describes the Preliminary Phase within the ADM. This can be thought of as the foundation for subsequent phases. Decision points in this phase include "How do we do architecture?", defining the framework and the key architecture principles.

— Chapter 5 describes Phase A: Architecture Vision. This phase sets the scope, constraints, and expectations for the project.

— Chapter 6 describes Phase B: Business Architecture. From the business perspective, a Baseline Architecture ("as is") is developed, as well as a Target Architecture ("to be"), and the gaps between them analyzed.

— Chapter 7 provides an introduction to Phase C: Information Systems Architectures, with the two following chapters going into the details of two parts of Phase C.

— Chapter 8 looks at Data Architecture within Phase C.

— Chapter 9 looks at Applications Architecture within Phase C.

— Chapter 10 looks at Phase D: Technology Architecture. The Technology Architecture is used as the basis of the following implementation work.

— Chapter 11 looks at Phase E: Opportunities and Solutions. This is the phase where major implementation projects are identified.

— Chapter 12 describes Phase F: Migration Planning. This phase analyzes the costs, benefits, and risks of proposed projects, and produces an implementation roadmap.

— Chapter 13 describes Phase G: Implementation Governance. This phase is to ensure that the implementation project conforms to the architecture.

— Chapter 14 describes Phase H: Architecture Change Management. This phase is to ensure that the architecture can respond to the needs of the enterprise as changes arise.

• Part 2: TOGAF VERSION 8.1.1 Architecture Development Model
  – Information Sets consists of a single chapter:
    — Chapter 15 describes the ADM Information Sets. These thirty topics comprise key components of the ADM and consist of checklists and guidelines.

- Part 3: TOGAF Foundation Architecture consists of two chapters:
  — Chapter 16 describes the Technical Reference Model (TRM).
  — Chapter 17 describes the Standards Information Base (SIB).
- Part 4: The Enterprise Continuum consists of three chapters:
  — Chapter 18 provides an overview of the Enterprise Continuum.
  — Chapter 19 describes the Architecture Continuum.
  — Chapter 20 describes the Solutions Continuum.
- Part 5: TOGAF and Other Architectures/Frameworks consists of a single chapter:
  — Chapter 21 compares TOGAF to other architectures and frameworks.
- Part 6: Architecture Governance consists of a single chapter:
  — Chapter 22 provides a high-level Introduction to governance and the TOGAF Architecture Governance Framework.
- Appendix A provides the answers to the Test Yourself sections provided at the end of each chapter.
- Appendix B provides a Test Yourself examination to allow you to assess your knowledge of TOGAF.
- Appendix C provides the answers to the examination in Appendix B.
- Appendix D provides the TOGAF 8 Certified Course Syllabus, including a mapping from each part of the syllabus to sections within this Study Guide.

How to Use this Study Guide

The chapters in this Study Guide are arranged to follow the organization of the TOGAF 8 Certified Course Syllabus (see Appendix D) and should be read in order. However, you may wish to use this Study Guide during revision of topics with which you are already familiar, and it is certainly possible to select topics for revision in any order. Where a topic requires further information from a later part in the syllabus, a cross-reference is provided.

Within each chapter are "Key Learning Points" and "Summary" sections that help you to easily identify what you need to know for each topic.

Each chapter has "Test Yourself" questions that will help you to test your understanding of the chapter and prepare for the TOGAF 8 Certified Examination. The purpose of these is to reinforce key learning points in the chapter. These are multiple-choice format questions where you must identify one correct answer.

Each chapter also has a "Recommended Reading" section that indicates the relevant sections in the TOGAF document that should be read to obtain a full understanding of the subject material. This is important since the TOGAF document contains much additional detailed material not included in this document.

Finally, at the end of this Study Guide is a "Test Yourself" examination paper that you can use to test your readiness to take the official TOGAF 8 Certified Examination.

Conventions Used in this Study Guide
The following conventions are used throughout this Study Guide in order to help identify important information and avoid confusion over the intended meaning.

- Ellipsis (…)
  Indicates a continuation; such as an incomplete list of example items, or a continuation from preceding text.
- **Bold**
  Used to highlight specific terms.
- *Italics*
  Used for emphasis. May also refer to other external documents.
- *(Syllabus reference x.y)*
  Used to identify text related to part of the TOGAF 8 Certified Course Syllabus, as detailed in Appendix D.

In addition to typographical conventions, the following conventions are used to highlight segments of text:

A Note box is used to highlight useful or interesting information.

A Tip box is used to provide key information that can save you time or that may not be entirely obvious.

About The Open Group

The Open Group is a vendor-neutral and technology-neutral consortium, whose vision of Boundaryless Information Flow™ will enable access to integrated information within and between enterprises based on open standards and global interoperability. The Open Group works with customers, suppliers, consortia, and other standards bodies. Its role is to capture, understand, and address current and emerging requirements, establish policies, and share best practices; to facilitate interoperability, develop consensus, and evolve and integrate specifications and Open Source technologies; to offer a comprehensive set of services to enhance the operational efficiency of consortia; and to operate the industry's premier certification service.

Further information on The Open Group is available at www.opengroup.org.

The Open Group has over 15 years' experience in developing and operating certification programs and has extensive experience developing and facilitating industry adoption of test suites used to validate conformance to an open standard or specification.

The Open Group publishes a wide range of technical documentation, the main part of which is focused on development of Technical and Product Standards and Guides, but which also includes White Papers, Technical Studies, and Business Titles.

A catalog is available at www.opengroup.org/bookstore.

About the Author

Rachel Harrison is Managing Director of Stratton Edge Consulting and a Visiting Professor of Computer Science at the University of Reading. Previously, she was Professor of Computer Science at the University of Reading, Head of the Department of Computer Science, Director of Research for the School of Systems Engineering, and Co-Founder and Director of the Reading e-Science Centre and of the Informatics Research Centre. Her research interests include software metrics, requirements engineering, systems evolution, and software testing. She has published over 80 refereed papers and consulted widely with industry, working with organizations such as IBM, the DRA, Philips Research Labs, Praxis Critical Systems, and The Open Group.

Prof. Harrison holds an MA in Mathematics from Oxford University, an MSc in Computer Science from University College London, and a PhD in Computer Science from the University of Southampton. She is a Member of the British Computer Society, an Affiliate Member of the IEEE-CS, a Member of the Association of Computing Machinery, and is a Chartered Engineer.

Acknowledgements

The Open Group gratefully acknowledges The Open Group Architecture Forum for developing The Open Group Architecture Framework (TOGAF).

The Open Group gratefully acknowledges the following reviewers who participated in the review of the TOGAF 8 Examination and this Study Guide:

Michael J. Aikins	Aslam Handy
Kazuhiko Arashima	Juergen Heck
Chris Blake	Judith Jones
Allen Brown	Andrew Josey
Lynne Canal	Robin Jourdan
Simon Dalziel	Graham Meaden
Soterol de Freitas	James R. Odrowski
William Estrem	Peter H. Sorensen
David Gilmour	John Spencer
Chris Greenslade	Jane Wadley-Varnus
Lian Guan	Amit Vohra
Arun Gupta	

References

The following documents and web links are referenced in this Study Guide:

- ANSI/IEEE Std 1471-2000, Recommended Practice for Architectural Description of Software-Intensive Systems.
- Architecture Trade-off Analysis Method (ATAM), Carnegie Mellon University, Software Engineering Institute (www.sei.cmu.edu/architecture/ata_method.html).
- Evaluating Software Architectures: Methods and Case Studies, P. Clements, R. Kazman, & M. Klein, 2002, Addison-Wesley.
- IEEE Std 1003.0-1995 Guide to the POSIX Open System Environment (OSE), identical to ISO/IEC TR 14252 (administratively withdrawn by IEEE).
- IEEE Std 1003.23-1998, Guide for Developing User Organization Open System Environment (OSE) Profiles (administratively withdrawn by IEEE).
- Information Technology Infrastructure Library (ITIL), UK Office of Government Commerce (www.itil.co.uk).
- Interoperable Enterprise Business Scenario, October 2002 (K022), published by The Open Group.
- ISO/IEC TR 14252:1996, Information Technology – Guide to the POSIX Open System Environment (OSE) (identical to IEEE Std 1003.0).
- Model Driven Architecture (MDA), Object Management Group (www.omg.org/mda).
- OECD Principles of Corporate Governance, Organization for Economic Co-operation and Development, December 2001 (www.oecd.org).
- The Open Group Architecture Framework (TOGAF) Version 8.1.1, Enterprise Edition, October 2007, ISBN 978 90 8753 094 5, published for The Open Group by Van Haren Publishing (see also www.vanharen.net).
- TOGAF Version 8.1, Enterprise Edition Corrigendum, July 2005 (U065), published by The Open Group.
- Volère Requirements Specification template (www.volere.co.uk).
- Zachman Framework, Zachman Institute for Framework Advancement (ZIFA) (www.zifa.com).

Introduction

1.1 Key Learning Points

This document is a Study Guide for TOGAF™ Version 8 Enterprise Edition for students planning to become TOGAF 8 Certified. It will familiarize you with all the materials that you need to know in order to pass the TOGAF 8 Certified Examination.

It gives an overview of every learning objective for the TOGAF 8 Certified Course Syllabus and in-depth coverage on preparing and taking the TOGAF 8 Certified Examination. It is specifically designed to help professional architects prepare for TOGAF 8 certification.

This first chapter will familiarize you with the TOGAF 8 certification program and its principles, as well as give you important information about the structure of the TOGAF 8 Certified Examination.

The objectives of this chapter are as follows:
- To provide an understanding of TOGAF certification and why you should become TOGAF 8 Certified
- To learn key facts about the TOGAF 8 Certified Examination

1.2 TOGAF Certification

TOGAF certification is required of individuals and suppliers who wish to use the TOGAF certification logo in association with their services and products.

The purpose of The Open Group TOGAF certification program is to ensure the consistent application and usage of TOGAF throughout the industry, and so protect the value of TOGAF for its users. A comprehensive introduction to the TOGAF certification program is available on The Open Group TOGAF certification web site at www.opengroup.org/togaf/cert.

Why is TOGAF certification important?
The existence of a certification program for TOGAF provides a strong incentive for organizations to standardize on TOGAF as the open method for enterprise IT architecture, and so avoid lock-in to proprietary methods. It is an important step in making enterprise IT architecture a well-recognized discipline, and in introducing rigor into the procurement of tools and services for enterprise architecture.

There are four different classes of certification within the TOGAF 8 certification program. These are termed "Product Standards" and are described as follows.

TOGAF 8 Certified is for individual IT architects. This certification acknowledges that an individual has a common core of knowledge and understanding of the TOGAF material through study and/or training. Individuals who are TOGAF Certified can provide services for organizations that are certified for TOGAF Professional Services and be instructors for certified TOGAF Training courses.

TOGAF 8 Training is for organizations providing training courses that instruct in TOGAF. This certification class ensures that the course syllabus includes coverage of the necessary elements of the applicable version of the TOGAF documentation and its Architecture Development Method. TOGAF Training courses are given by instructors who themselves are TOGAF Certified.

TOGAF 8 Professional Services is for organizations that offer professional services in support of TOGAF. This certification ensures that organizations that offer such services abide by an approved code of practice, and use only TOGAF Certified architects for such services.

TOGAF 8
Tool Support

TOGAF 8 Tool Support is for organizations that provide architecture tools that support TOGAF. This certification ensures that the meaning of a claim of conformance with the TOGAF documentation is clear and that the TOGAF Architecture Development Method is supported consistently.

It is possible for an organization to be involved in the TOGAF certification program in several of the classes simultaneously; for example, an individual can be TOGAF Certified and employed by an organization that is certified for one or more of TOGAF Tool Support, TOGAF Training, and TOGAF Professional Services.

This Study Guide concentrates on the first certification class above – TOGAF Certified. For TOGAF 8 Enterprise Edition, this is TOGAF 8 Certified.

What is a Product Standard?

A Product Standard is a precisely defined and documented set of functionality against which products, services, or individuals may be certified.

Each Product Standard document includes a description of the nature and purpose of the Product Standard, detailed technical Conformance Requirements, specific prerequisite requirements that must be satisfactorily completed, supporting information (if any), and, if applicable, a summary of the migration issues to the current Product Standard from previous versions of the Product Standard.

Source: TOGAF Certification Policy, Version 1.1 (X050)

Why Become TOGAF 8 Certified?

Becoming TOGAF 8 Certified demonstrates clearly to employers and peers your commitment to enterprise architecture as a discipline. In particular, it demonstrates that you possess a body of core knowledge about TOGAF 8 as an open, industry standard framework and method for enterprise architecture. The Open Group publishes the definitive register of TOGAF 8 Certified individuals, and certified service and product offerings, and issues certificates. TOGAF certification for individuals also includes an entitlement for free membership in the Association of Open Group Enterprise Architects (www.aogea.org).

1.2.1 TOGAF Certification Principles

The Open Group Architecture Forum established the following principles when developing the TOGAF certification program:

Table 1.1: TOGAF Certification Principles

Motivators to Operate TOGAF Certification	Certification Goals	Certification Aspects
Create trust by clients in TOGAF	Match client's requirements	Syllabus and examination are geared towards knowledge required in practice, not academic. Certification eases contracting for architecture work.
	Integrity	Examination is uniform and repeatable.
Protect architects' learning investment	Objectivity	Criteria and procedures minimize subjectivity.
	Scalability	Examination and supporting training services are easily scalable while protecting integrity.
	International recognition	Certified architects are recognized internationally.
	Value recognition	Certification improves employability and marketability.
Grow and maintain a positive image of TOGAF	Promote brand	Policy, processes, and criteria are robust and efficient, creating a positively trusted image.
	High share of architecture profession	Certification and training services are easily available around the world.

1.2.2 TOGAF 8 Certified

The TOGAF 8 Certified class defines the core requirements for knowledge and awareness of TOGAF 8.1 that IT architecture practitioners should have in order to be able to use TOGAF 8.1 effectively in developing IT architectures. It is the foundation for other TOGAF 8 certification classes, and is required for architects delivering certified TOGAF 8 Training courses and certified TOGAF 8 Professional Services.

Once certified, individuals have an entry on the public certification register, which lists their name, company, registration and expiry dates, and a link to download a certificate. Figure 1-1 shows a mockup of the register with fictional entries.

Individual (see details)	Company	▲ First Registered	▲ Expires ▼	Certificate
Chris Aardvark	Aardvark Computers	21-Nov-2003	21-Nov-2007	
Ethan Bennett	Clayface	11-Jul-2006	11-Jul-2009	
June Edwards	Acme Industry Inc.	28-Oct-2005	28-Oct-2007	
Lilly Pink	LP Company	31-Jan-2006	31-Jan-2008	
Andrew Sample	Open Goop	03-Feb-2006	03-Feb-2008	
John Smith	The Oden Group	08-Jun-2006	08-Jun-2008	

Figure 1.1: TOGAF 8 Certified Register Extract (Sample)

A sample certificate is shown in Figure 1-2.

1.2.3 The Certification Process

This Study Guide is aimed at preparing you to become TOGAF 8 Certified through the examination route. The TOGAF 8 Certified Examination comprises 101 multiple-choice questions that must be completed within two hours.

The TOGAF 8 Certified Course Syllabus for the examination is available within the TOGAF 8 Training Conformance Statement[1]. A mapping of the TOGAF 8 Certified Course Syllabus to the sections of this Study Guide is contained in Appendix D.

The six topic areas covered by the examination together with the approximate percentage of the number of questions in the examination follows:
1. TOGAF 8 Architecture Development Method (ADM) – Process (50%)
2. TOGAF 8 Architecture Development Method (ADM) – Information Sets (25%)

---

[1] Refer to www.opengroup.org/togaf/cert/docs/togaf8certdocs/TOGAF_8_TRAINING_CSQ.htm.

This certifies that

Andrew Sample

has successfully achieved the standards for TOGAF 8 Certification
indicating conformance to the TOGAF 8 Certification Program,
as established by The Open Group.

Date registered: *03 February 2006*
Valid until: *03 February 2008*

Registration Number: 101

Allen Brown, President and CEO, The Open Group

THE *Open* GROUP

Figure 1.2: TOGAF 8 Certified Certificate

3. TOGAF Foundation Architecture (5%)
4. The Enterprise Continuum (8%)
5. TOGAF and Other Architectures/Frameworks (4%)
6. Architecture Governance (8%)

1.2.3.1   Format of the Examination Questions

The examination questions are multiple-choice questions. These are very
similar in format to the Test Yourself questions included in each chapter.
Note that the exact format for display is test center-specific and will be made
clear on the screens when taking the examination.

1.2.3.2 What do I need to bring with me to take the Examination?

You should consult with the examination center regarding the forms of picture ID you are required to bring with you to verify your identification.

1.2.3.3 Can I refer to materials while I take the Examination?

No; it is a closed-book examination.

1.2.3.4 If I fail, how soon can I retake the Examination?

You should consult the current policy on The Open Group web site. At the time of writing, the policy states that individuals who have failed the examination are not be allowed to retake the examination within 30 days of the first sitting, and have no more than three attempts in twelve months.

1.2.4 Preparing for the Examination

You can prepare for the examination by working through this Study Guide section-by-section. A mapping of the sections of this Study Guide to the TOGAF 8 Certified Course Syllabus is given in Appendix D. After completing each section, you should answer the Test Yourself questions and read the referenced sections from the TOGAF documentation. Once you have completed all the sections in this Study Guide, you can then attempt the Test Yourself examination paper in Appendix B. The sample paper uses an extended multiple-choice format asking you to select true or false to a number of statements in each knowledge area. This is designed to give a thorough test of your knowledge. If you have completed all the prescribed preparation and can attain a pass mark for the Test Yourself examination paper as described in Appendix C, then it is likely you are ready to sit the examination.

1.3 Summary

The TOGAF certification program has four Product Standards for TOGAF 8. A Product Standard defines a class against which an individual, product, or organization can become certified. The individual class for certification for TOGAF 8 is known as "TOGAF 8 Certified".

The topic for this Study Guide is preparation for taking the TOGAF 8 Certified Examination. The examination comprises 101 multiple-choice questions to be completed in two hours. A large part of the examination is based upon the TOGAF Architecture Development method (ADM).

Preparing for the examination includes the following steps:

- You should work through this Study Guide step-by-step.
- At the end of each chapter, you should complete the Test Yourself questions and read the sections of the TOGAF documentation listed under Recommended Reading.
- Once you have completed all the chapters in this Study Guide, you should attempt the "Test Yourself" examination paper given in Appendix C.
- If you can attain the target score in Appendix D, then you have completed your preparation.

1.4 Test Yourself Questions

Q1:   TOGAF certification is available for how many classes of "Product Standards"?
   A.   5
   B.   4
   C.   3
   D.   8
   E.   6

Q2:   Which one of the following TOGAF certification Product Standards is for individual architects?
   A.   TOGAF 8 Certified
   B.   TOGAF 8 Professional Services
   C.   TOGAF 8 Tool Support
   D.   TOGAF 8 Training

Q3:   TOGAF Training certification is applicable to:
   A.   Individuals who will be giving TOGAF Training courses
   B.   Organizations who have a TOGAF Training course
   C.   Individuals who have successfully completed a TOGAF Training course
   D.   All of these
   E.   Other

Q4:   Which of the following statements best describes the three goals of the TOGAF certification program?
   A.   Integrity, Scalability, Flexibility
   B.   Objectivity, Robustness, Simplicity

    C.   Scalability, Objectivity, Integrity
    D.   Knowledge-based, Valuable, Simplicity
    E.   All of these

Q5:   Which of the following topic areas is not included in the TOGAF 8 Certified Course Syllabus?
    A.   The TOGAF Foundation Architecture
    B.   The Enterprise Continuum
    C.   Architecture Governance
    D.   The Integrated Information Infrastructure Reference Model
    E.   Gap Analysis

Q6:   Which of the following does not apply to the TOGAF 8 Certified Examination?
    A.   Candidates who fail cannot take the examination again within 30 days.
    B.   No candidate is allowed to attempt the same examination more than three times in 12 months.
    C.   The examination consists of more than 100 questions.
    D.   The examination has multiple-choice format questions.
    E.   It is an open-book examination.

1.5 Recommended Reading

The following are recommended sources of further information for this chapter:

- TOGAF Certification Policy, Version 1.1, October 2005 (X050), published by The Open Group (www.opengroup.org/bookstore/catalog/x050.htm)
- TOGAF 8 Certified Product Standard, October 2005 (X05TA), published by The Open Group (www.opengroup.org/bookstore/catalog/x05ta.htm)
- The Open Group TOGAF Certification web site: www.opengroup.org/togaf/cert

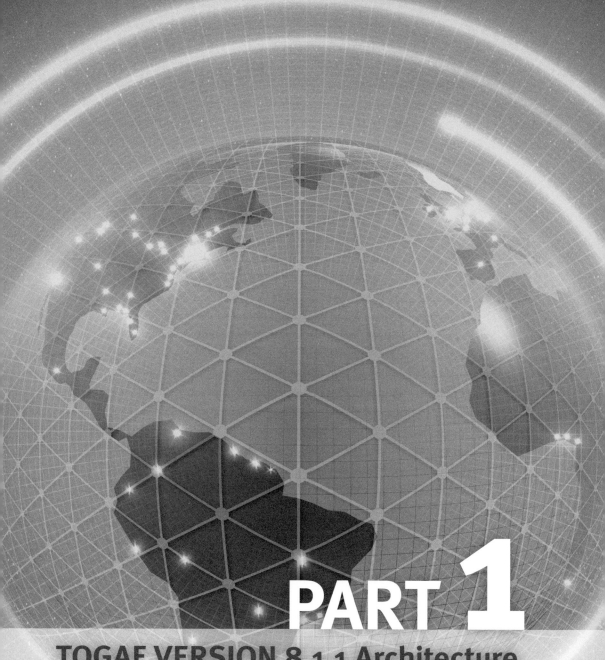

PART 1

TOGAF VERSION 8.1.1 Architecture
Development Method (ADM)
Process

Chapter 2

TOGAF Version 8.1.1 Overview

2.1 Key Learning Points

This chapter will familiarize you with the TOGAF fundamentals that you need to know to pass the TOGAF 8 Certified Examination. The objectives of this chapter are as follows:

- To provide an introduction to TOGAF 8

Key Points Explained

This chapter will help you to answer the following questions:

- What is an enterprise? What is enterprise architecture?
- What is architecture in the context of TOGAF?
- What is an architecture framework?
- Why do I need a framework for enterprise architecture?
- What specifically does TOGAF contain?
- What kind of "architecture" are we talking about?
- What kind of architecture does TOGAF deal with?

TOGAF emphasizes business goals as architecture drivers, and provides a repository of best practice. It includes the TOGAF Architecture Development Method (ADM), a meticulous iterative approach to planning, designing, realizing, and governing the architecture. In addition, reference architectures that provide a set of templates for an organization to adapt to their specific requirements, and finally a resource base.

Bill Estrem, "TOGAF to the Rescue" (www.opengroup.org/downloads)

2.2 Introduction to TOGAF

TOGAF is an architecture framework – The Open Group Architecture Framework.

TOGAF is developed and maintained by The Open Group Architecture Forum. The first version of TOGAF, developed in 1995, was based on the US

Department of Defense Technical Architecture Framework for Information Management (TAFIM). Starting from this sound foundation, The Open Group Architecture Forum has developed successive versions of TOGAF at regular intervals and published each one on The Open Group public web site.

This Study Guide covers TOGAF 8.1, including TOGAF 8.1.1. TOGAF 8.1 was first published in December 2003, with a minor revision in 2006 to address defects, known as TOGAF 8.1.1.

TOGAF can be used for developing a broad range of different IT architectures. TOGAF complements, and can be used in conjunction with, other frameworks that are more focused on specific deliverables for particular vertical sectors such as Government, Defense, and Finance. The key to TOGAF is the method – the TOGAF Architecture Development Method – for developing an IT architecture that addresses business needs.

When appropriate, this Study Guide contains references to sections within TOGAF, which are referred to as "the TOGAF document". The references are intended to be functional for both the web version and printed versions of the document. Therefore, the format of the reference number contains both the Part and the Chapter name, but not the Chapter number and page references since they exist only in the printed book.

2.2.1   Structure of the TOGAF Document
The following table summarizes the four parts of the TOGAF document:

2.2.2   What is an Enterprise? What is Enterprise Architecture?
TOGAF defines an "enterprise" as any collection of organizations that has a common set of goals. For example, an enterprise could be a government agency, a whole corporation, a division of a corporation, a single department, or a chain of geographically distant organizations linked together by common ownership.

Table 2.1: Structure of the TOGAF Document

Part I: Introduction	This part provides a high-level introduction to some of the key concepts behind enterprise architecture and in particular the TOGAF approach.
Part II: Architecture Development Method	This is the core of TOGAF. It describes the TOGAF Architecture Development Method (ADM) – a step-by-step approach to development of an enterprise architecture.
Part III: Enterprise Continuum	This part describes the TOGAF Enterprise Continuum, a virtual repository of architecture assets, which includes the TOGAF Foundation Architecture, and the Integrated Information Infrastructure Reference Model (III-RM).
Part IV: Resources	This part comprises the TOGAF Resource Base – a set of tools and techniques available for use in applying TOGAF and the TOGAF ADM.

The term "enterprise" in the context of "enterprise architecture" can be used to denote both an entire enterprise, encompassing all of its information systems, and a specific domain within the enterprise. In both cases, the architecture crosses multiple systems and multiple functional groups within the enterprise.

Confusion often arises from the evolving nature of the term "enterprise". An extended enterprise nowadays frequently includes partners, suppliers, and customers. If the goal is to integrate an extended enterprise, then the enterprise comprises the partners, suppliers, and customers, as well as internal business units.

For example, an organization with an online store that uses an external fulfillment house for dispatching orders would extend its definition of the enterprise in that system to include the fulfillment house.

2.2.3 What is Architecture in the Context of TOGAF?

ANSI/IEEE Std 1471-2000 defines "architecture" as:

"The fundamental organization of a system, embodied in its components, their relationships to each other and the environment, and the principles governing its design and evolution."

TOGAF embraces but does not strictly adhere to ANSI/IEEE Std 1471-2000 terminology. In TOGAF, "architecture" has two meanings depending upon the context:

1. A formal description of a system, or a detailed plan of the system at a component level to guide its implementation
2. The structure of components, their inter-relationships, and the principles and guidelines governing their design and evolution over time

2.2.4 What is an Architecture Framework?

An architecture framework is a tool that can be used for developing a broad range of different architectures. It should describe a method for designing an information system in terms of a set of building blocks, and for showing how the building blocks fit together. It should contain a set of tools and provide a common vocabulary. It should also include a list of recommended standards and compliant products that can be used to implement the building blocks.

2.2.5 Why do I need a Framework for Enterprise Architecture?

Using an architecture framework will speed up and simplify architecture development, ensure more complete coverage of the designed solution, and make certain that the architecture selected allows for future growth in response to the needs of the business. Architecture design is a technically complex process, and the design of heterogeneous, multi-vendor architectures is particularly complex. TOGAF plays an important role in helping to "de-mystify" the architecture development process, enabling IT users to build genuinely open systems-based solutions to their business needs.

Regulatory Drivers for Adoption of Enterprise Architecture

There are a number of laws and regulations that have been drivers for the adoption and use of enterprise architecture in business:

- The Clinger-Cohen Act
  (US Information Technology Management Reform Act 1996)
  The Information Technology Reform Act (Clinger-Cohen Act) is designed to improve the way the US Federal Government acquires and manages information technology. It mandates the use of a formal enterprise architecture process for all US federal agencies.

- The Sarbanes-Oxley Act

  (US Public Company Accounting Reform and Investor Protection Act 2002)

  The Sarbanes-Oxley Act was passed in response to a number of major corporate and accounting scandals involving prominent companies in the United States (for example, Enron and Worldcom). Under the Act, companies must provide attestation of internal control assessment, including documentation of control procedures related to information technology.

- EU Directives on the Award of Public Contracts

  Similarly within the European Union, there are EU Directives that require vendors involved in Public Contracts to show that they are using formal enterprise architecture processes within their businesses when supplying products and services.

2.2.6 What kind of Architecture does TOGAF deal with?

TOGAF 8.1.1 covers the development of four related types of architecture. These four types of architecture are commonly accepted as subsets of an overall enterprise architecture, all of which TOGAF is designed to support. They are as follows:

Table 2.2: Architecture Types Supported by TOGAF

Architecture Type	Description
Business (or Business Process) Architecture	This defines the business strategy, governance, organization, and key business processes.
Data Architecture	This describes the structure of an organization's logical and physical data assets and data management resources.
Applications Architecture	This kind of architecture provides a blueprint for the individual application systems to be deployed, their interactions, and their relationships to the core business processes of the organization.
Technology Architecture	This describes the logical software and hardware capabilities that are required to support the deployment of business, data, and application services. This includes IT infrastructure, middleware, networks, communications, processing, and standards.

2.2.7   What Specifically does TOGAF Contain?

TOGAF consists of three main parts:

1. The TOGAF Architecture Development Method (ADM)
2. The Enterprise Continuum
3. The TOGAF Resource Base

2.2.7.1   The TOGAF Architecture Development Method (ADM)

The TOGAF Architecture Development Method (ADM) explains how to derive an organization-specific enterprise architecture that addresses business requirements. The ADM provides:

- A reliable, proven way of developing the architecture
- Architecture views that enable the architect to ensure that a complex set of requirements are adequately addressed
- Linkages to practical case studies
- Guidelines on tools for architecture development

2.2.7.2   The Enterprise Continuum

The Enterprise Continuum is a "virtual repository" of all the architecture assets – models, patterns, architecture descriptions, etc. – that exist both within the enterprise and in the IT industry at large, and which the enterprise can use for the development of architectures. At relevant places throughout the TOGAF ADM, there are reminders to consider which architecture assets the architect should use.

TOGAF itself provides two reference models for possible inclusion in an enterprise's own Enterprise Continuum:

Table 2.3: Reference Models included in the Enterprise Continuum

Reference Model	Description
The TOGAF Foundation Architecture; see Chapter 16	The TOGAF Foundation Architecture is an architecture of generic services and functions that provides a foundation on which specific architectures and Architecture Building Blocks (ABBs) can be built. This Foundation Architecture in turn includes: • The TOGAF Technical Reference Model (TRM), which provides a model and taxonomy of generic platform services • The TOGAF Standards Information Base (SIB) (see Chapter 17) which is a database of open industry standards that can be used to define the particular services and other components of an enterprise-specific architecture

Reference Model	Description
The Integrated Information Infrastructure Reference Model (III-RM)	The Integrated Information Infrastructure Reference Model (III-RM) is based on the TOGAF Foundation Architecture, and is specifically aimed at helping the design of architectures that enable and support the vision of Boundaryless Information Flow.

III-RM

The Open Group has documented the business scenario that led to the creation of the Integrated Information Infrastructure Reference Model (III-RM) in the Interoperable Enterprise Business Scenario (K022). This is freely available for download from the Business Scenarios section of The Open Group online bookstore at www.opengroup.org/bookstore.

2.2.7.3   The TOGAF Resource Base

The final part of the TOGAF 8.1.1 document is the TOGAF Resource Base, which is a set of resources, guidelines, templates, background information, etc. provided to be of assistance to the architect in the use of the ADM. The resources include:

- Architecture Board: Guidelines for establishing and operating an enterprise Architecture Board.
- Architecture Compliance: Guidelines for ensuring project compliance to architecture.
- Architecture Contracts: Guidelines for defining and using Architecture Contracts.
- Architecture Governance: Framework and guidelines for architecture governance.
- Architecture Maturity Models: Techniques for evaluating and quantifying an organization's maturity in enterprise architecture.
- Architecture Patterns: Guidelines for using architectural patterns.
- Architecture Principles: Principles for the use and deployment of IT resources across the enterprise.
- Architecture Skills Framework: A set of role, skill, and experience norms for staff undertaking enterprise architecture work.
- Architecture Views: Guidelines for viewpoints and views in architecture models.

- Building Blocks Example: A fictional example illustrating building blocks in architecture.
- Business Process Domain Views: A set of function views aligned with the business process structure of the enterprise.
- Business Scenarios: A method for deriving business requirements for architecture and the implied technical requirements.
- Case Studies: Real-life examples of TOGAF in use.
- Glossary: Definitions of key terms.
- Other Architectures/Frameworks: Other frameworks and their relationship to TOGAF.
- Tools for Architecture Development: Tools and techniques helpful in using TOGAF.
- Zachman Framework Mapping: Mapping the TOGAF ADM to the Zachman Framework.

2.3 Summary

What is an enterprise?
- A collection of organizations that share a common set of goals, such as a government agency, part of a corporation, or a corporation in its entirety
- Large corporations may comprise multiple enterprises
- An "extended enterprise" can include partners, suppliers, and customers

What is an architecture?
An architecture is the fundamental organization of something, embodied in its components, their relationships to each other and the environment, and the principles governing its design and evolution.

TOGAF is an architecture framework, "The Open Group Architecture Framework". It enables you to design, evaluate, and build the right architecture for your organization. An architecture framework is a toolkit that can be used for developing a broad range of different architectures.
- It should describe a method for designing an information system in terms of a set of building blocks, and for showing how the building blocks fit together.
- It should contain a set of tools and provide a common vocabulary.
- It should also include a list of recommended standards and compliant products that can be used to implement the building blocks.

The value of a framework is that it provides a practical starting point for an architecture project.

The components of TOGAF 8.1.1 are as follows:
- Architecture Development Method (ADM)
- The Enterprise Continuum
- The TOGAF Resource Base

2.4 Test Yourself Questions

Q1:   Which of the following statements best describes TOGAF?
    A.   TOGAF is a tool for developing Technology Architectures only.
    B.   TOGAF is an architecture framework and method for architecture development.
    C.   TOGAF is a business model.
    D.   TOGAF is a specific architecture pattern.

Q2:   Why do you need a framework for enterprise architecture?
    A.   Architecture design is complex.
    B.   Using a framework can speed up the process.
    C.   Using a framework ensures more complete coverage.
    D.   A framework provides a set of tools and a common vocabulary.
    E.   All of these

Q3:   Which of the following is not considered one of the three main parts of TOGAF?
    A.   The Architecture Development Method
    B.   The Enterprise Continuum
    C.   The Technical Reference Model
    D.   The TOGAF Resource Base

Q4:   Which of the types of IT architecture below is not commonly accepted as part of the enterprise architecture addressed by TOGAF?
    A.   Business Architecture
    B.   Data Architecture
    C.   Applications Architecture
    D.   Technology Architecture
    E.   Pattern Architecture

Q5:   The Enterprise Continuum is:
    A. An architecture framework
    B. A database of open industry standards
    C. A technical reference model
    D. A virtual repository of architecture assets
    E. A method for developing architectures

2.5 Recommended Reading

The following are recommended sources of further information for this chapter:

- TOGAF 8.1.1 Enterprise Edition Part I: Introduction, Introduction and TOGAF as an Enterprise Architecture

Chapter 3

Introduction to the Architecture Development Method

3.1 Key Learning Points

This chapter describes the Architecture Development Method (ADM), what it is, its relationship to the rest of TOGAF, and high-level considerations for its use.

Key Points Explained

This chapter will help you to answer the following questions:

- What is the TOGAF ADM?
- What is its relationship to other parts of TOGAF?
- What are the phases of the TOGAF ADM?
- How can I adapt the ADM to my enterprise?
- How can I scope the architecture activity for my organization?
- How can I integrate the architecture domains for my organization?
- What are the expected inputs and outputs to the ADM?
- How do I manage requirements during the ADM cycle?
- How do I use the TOGAF Resource Base during the ADM cycle?

Key Fact

Why is TOGAF becoming so popular in the industry?

One key reason is that architects can use the TOGAF ADM in conjunction with any of the popular frameworks.

The TOGAF ADM is framework-agnostic, and helps IT architects fill in the framework they might already have in use.

Bill Estrem, "TOGAF to the Rescue" (www.opengroup.org/downloads)

3.2 What is the TOGAF ADM?

The Architecture Development Method (ADM), which forms the core of TOGAF, is a method for deriving organization-specific enterprise architecture and is the result of contributions from many architecture practitioners. It is specifically designed to address business requirements. The ADM provides:

- A reliable, proven way of developing the architecture
- A set of architecture views (business, applications, data, technology) that enable the architect to ensure that a complex set of requirements are adequately addressed
- Linkages to practical case studies
- Guidelines on tools for architecture development

The TOGAF ADM defines a recommended sequence for the various phases and steps involved in developing an organization-wide enterprise architecture, but the ADM cannot determine scope: this must be determined by the organization itself.

3.3 What is its Relationship to Other Parts of TOGAF?

There are two other main parts to TOGAF, besides the ADM: the Enterprise Continuum and the TOGAF Resource Base.

The Enterprise Continuum, described in detail in this document in Part 4, The Enterprise Continuum (see Chapter 19), can be thought of as a "framework-within-a-framework" that provides context for the leveraging of relevant architecture assets and provides navigational help when discussions move between different levels of abstraction.

The TOGAF Resource Base (see Section 2.2.7.3), described in detail in TOGAF 8.1.1, Part IV: Resource Base, is a set of resources that is used to support the ADM. These resources include guidelines, templates, checklists, and other detailed materials.

3.4 What are the Phases of the ADM?

The ADM consists of a number of phases that cycle through a range of architecture views that enable the architect to ensure that a complex set of requirements are adequately addressed. The basic structure of the ADM is shown in Figure 3-1.

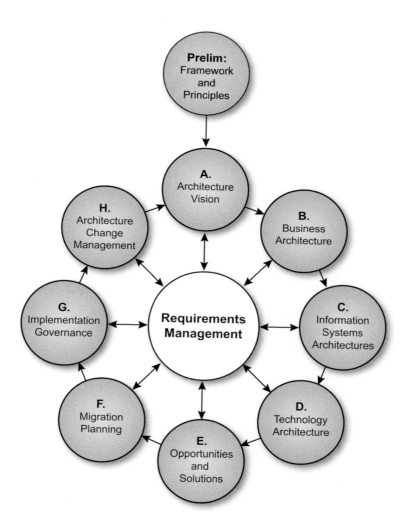

Figure 3.1: Architecture Development Cycle

It is an iterative process, over the whole process, between phases and within phases. Throughout the ADM cycle, there should be frequent validation of results against the original expectations, both those for the whole ADM cycle, and those for the particular phase of the process. Such validation should reconsider scope, detail, schedules, and milestones. Each phase should consider assets produced from previous iterations of the process and external assets from the marketplace, such as other frameworks or models.

There is a Preliminary Phase for project establishment followed by Phases A to H. These phases are examined in detail in the following chapters of this Study Guide.

Table 3-1 summarizes the activities of each ADM phase.

Table 3.1: Architecture Development Method Activities by Phase

Activity	ADM Phase
Prepare the organization for successful TOGAF architecture projects	Preliminary Phase: Framework & Principles (see Chapter 4)
Every stage of a TOGAF project should be based on and validate business requirements	Requirements Management (see Section 3.9)
Set the scope, constraints, and expectations for a TOGAF project Validate the business context and create the Statement of Architecture Work	Phase A: Architecture Vision (see Chapter 5)
Develop architectures at three levels 1. Business 2. Information Systems 3. Technology In each case develop the Baseline ("as is") and Target ("to be") Architecture and analyze gaps	Phase B: Business Architecture (see Chapter 6) Phase C: Information Systems Architectures (see Chapter 7) Phase D: Technology Architecture (see Chapter 10)
Identify major implementation projects	Phase E: Opportunities and Solutions (see Chapter 11)
Analyze cost benefits and risk Produce implementation roadmap	Phase F: Migration Planning (see Chapter 12)
Architecture Contracts are prepared and issued by the Implementation Governance Board to ensure that the implementation project conforms to the architecture	Phase G: Implementation Governance (see Chapter 13)

Activity	ADM Phase
Ensure that the architecture responds to the needs of the enterprise	Phase H: Architecture Change Management (see Chapter 14)

The phases of the ADM cycle shown in Architecture Development Cycle can then be further divided into steps as shown in Figure 3-2 that depicts the expansion of the Technology Architecture phase.

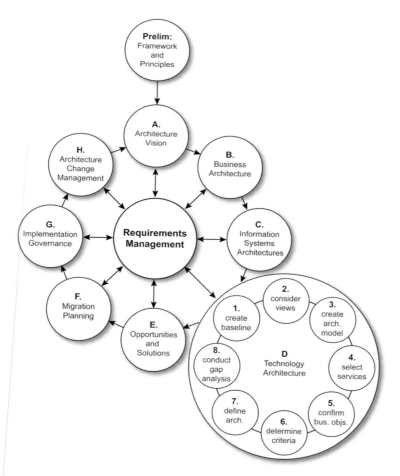

Figure 3.2: Architecture Development Cycle Expansion

3.5 How to Adapt the ADM to your Enterprise

The ADM is a generic method. It is designed to deal with most system and organizational requirements. It easily copes with variable geographies, vertical sectors, and industry types. However, it will usually be necessary to modify or extend the ADM, to suit specific needs. More information on Adapting the ADM is given in Chapter 4.

3.6 Scoping the Architecture Activity for your Organization

There are many reasons for wanting to limit the scope of the architecture activity to be undertaken, most of which come down to the availability of people, finance, and other resources. The scope chosen for the architecture activity is normally directly dependent on available resources, and, in the final analysis, is usually a question of feasibility.

Table 3-2 shows the four dimensions in which the scope may be defined and limited.

Table 3.2: Dimensions for Limiting the Scope of the Architecture Activity

Dimension	Considerations
Enterprise scope or focus	What is the full extent of the enterprise, and how much of that extent should the architecting effort focus on? Many enterprises are very large, effectively comprising a federation of organizational units that could validly be considered enterprises in their own right. The modern enterprise increasingly extends beyond its traditional boundaries, to embrace a fuzzy combination of traditional business enterprise combined with suppliers, customers, and partners.
Architecture domains	A complete enterprise architecture description should contain all four architecture domains (Business, Data, Applications, Technology), but the realities of resource and time constraints often mean there is not enough time, funding, or resources to build a top-down, all-inclusive architecture description encompassing all four architecture domains, even if the enterprise scope is chosen to be less than the full extent of the overall enterprise.
Vertical scope, or level of detail	To what level of detail should the architecting effort go? How much architecture is "enough"? What is the appropriate demarcation between the architecture effort and other, related activities (system design, system engineering, system development)?

Dimension	Considerations
Time horizon	What is the time horizon that needs to be articulated for the Architecture Vision, and does it make sense (in terms of practicality and resources) for the same horizon to be covered in the detailed architecture description? If not, how many intermediate Target Architectures are to be defined, and what are their time horizons?

3.7 Integrating the Architecture Domains for your Organization

There is a need to integrate the architecture domains identified by the phases of the ADM. This can be done by using an "enterprise framework" such as Zachman to position the various domains and artifacts, or by using a meta-architecture framework (i.e., principles, models, and standards) to allow interoperability, migration, and conformance between federated architectures.

A significant number of scoping decisions need to be taken, in terms of enterprise focus, architecture scope, level of detail, time horizons, and whether to define intermediate so-called "Transitional Architectures", any one of which may result in a less than complete architecture description being developed. A potential way of assessing the gaps in scope or level of detail is to use an enterprise architecture framework (e.g., Zachman) to understand the coverage of the artifacts.

As organizations address common themes (such as service-oriented architecture, and integrated information infrastructure), and universal data models and standard data structures emerge, integration toward the high end of the spectrum will be facilitated. However, there will always be the need for effective standards governance to reduce the need for manual co-ordination and conflict resolution.

3.8 ADM Inputs and Outputs

There are a number of input and output items referenced in the ADM. Table 3-3 provides a list of them. The list of outputs produced is a suggestion and need not be followed exactly. Each document produced should be versioned to indicate when a change has occurred as a result of execution of a phase within the ADM. The version numbering shown is also a suggestion and need not be followed exactly.

Table 3.3: ADM Inputs and Outputs by Phase

ADM Phase	Inputs	Outputs
Preliminary Phase: Framework & Principles (see Chapter 4)	TOGAF Architecture Development Method (ADM) Other architecture framework(s) Business strategy (including goals and drivers) IT governance strategy Architecture principles, including business principles Other federated architectures principles	Architecture principles Framework definition Restatement of business principles, goals, and drivers
Phase A: Architecture Vision (see Chapter 5)	Request for Architecture Work Business strategy, business goals, and business drivers Architecture principles, including business principles Enterprise Continuum; that is, existing architecture documentation (framework description, architecture descriptions, existing baseline descriptions, etc.)	Approved Statement of Architecture Work Refined statements of business goals and strategic drivers Architecture principles, including business principles Architecture Vision including: • Baseline Business Architecture, Version 0.1 • Baseline Technology Architecture, Version 0.1 • Baseline Data Architecture, Version 0.1 • Baseline Applications Architecture, Version 0.1 • Target Business Architecture, Version 0.1 • Target Technology Architecture, Version 0.1 • Target Data Architecture, Version 0.1 • Target Applications Architecture, Version 0.1

ADM Phase	Inputs	Outputs

Phase B:
Business Architecture
(see Chapter 6)
	Request for Architecture Work
	Approved Statement of
	Architecture Work
	Refined statements of business
	goals and strategic drivers
	Architecture principles, including
	business principles
	Enterprise Continuum
	Architecture Vision, including:
	• Baseline Business Architecture,
	  Version 0.1
	• Baseline Technology
	  Architecture, Version 0.1
	• Baseline Data Architecture,
	  Version 0.1
	• Baseline Applications
	  Architecture, Version 0.1
	• Target Business Architecture,
	  Version 0.1
	• Target Technology Architecture,
	  Version 0.1
	• Target Data Architecture,
	  Version 0.1
	• Target Applications Architecture,
	  Version 0.1
		Statement of Architecture Work,
		updated if necessary
		Validated business principles,
		business goals, and strategic
		drivers
		Target Business Architecture,
		Version 1.0 (detailed)
		Baseline Business Architecture,
		Version 1.0 (detailed)
		Views corresponding to the
		selected viewpoints addressing
		key stakeholder concerns
		Gap analysis results
		Technical requirements
		Business Architecture Report
		Updated business requirements

Phase C: Information Systems Architectures (see Chapter 7, Chapter 8, and Chapter 9)	Application Principles, if existing Data Principles, if existing Request for Architecture Work Statement of Architecture Work Architecture Vision Enterprise Continuum Baseline Business Architecture, Version 1.0 Target Business Architecture, Version 1.0 Baseline Data Architecture, Version 0.1 Target Data Architecture, Version 0.1 Baseline Applications Architecture, Version 0.1 Target Applications Architecture, Version 0.1 Relevant technical requirements that apply to Phase C Gap analysis results (from Business Architecture) Re-usable building blocks (from organization's Architecture Continuum)	Statement of Architecture Work, updated if necessary Baseline Data Architecture, Version 1.0 Target Data Architecture, Version 1.0 Baseline Applications Architecture, Version 1.0 Target Applications Architecture, Version 1.0 Data Architecture views Applications Architecture views Data Architecture Report, summarizing what was done and the key findings Applications Architecture Report, summarizing what was done and the key findings Gap analysis results Impact Analysis Updated business requirements

ADM Phase	Inputs	Outputs
Phase D: Technology Architecture (see Chapter 10)	Technology Principles, if existing Request for Architecture Work Statement of Architecture Work Architecture Vision Relevant technical requirements from previous phases Gap analysis results (from Data Architecture) Gap analysis results (from Applications Architecture) Baseline Business Architecture, Version 1.0 (detailed) Baseline Data Architecture, Version 1.0 Baseline Applications Architecture, Version 1.0 Target Business Architecture, Version 1.0 (detailed) Re-usable building blocks, from organization's Enterprise Continuum Target Data Architecture, Version 1.0 Target Applications Architecture, Version 1.0	Statement of Architecture Work, updated if necessary Baseline Technology Architecture, Version 1.0 Validated technology principles, or new technology principles (if generated here) Technology Architecture Report, summarizing what was done and the key findings Target Technology Architecture, Version 1.0 Technology Architecture, gap analysis results Viewpoints addressing key stakeholder concerns Views corresponding to the selected viewpoints
Phase E: Opportunities and Solutions (see Chapter 11)	Request for Architecture Work Statement of Architecture Work Target Business Architecture, Version 1.0 Target Data Architecture, Version 1.0 Target Applications Architecture, Version 1.0 Target Technology Architecture, Version 1.0 Re-usable Architecture Building Blocks (from organization's Enterprise Continuum) Product information	Implementation and migration strategy High-level Implementation Plan Impact Analysis – project list

ADM Phase	Inputs	Outputs
Phase F: Migration Planning (see Chapter 12)	Request for Architecture Work Statement of Architecture Work Target Business Architecture, Version 1.0 Target Data Architecture, Version 1.0 Target Applications Architecture, Version 1.0 Target Technology Architecture, Version 1.0 Impact Analysis – project list	Impact Analysis – detailed Implementation Plan and Migration Plan (including Architecture Implementation Contract)
Phase G: Implementation Governance (see Chapter 13)	Request for Architecture Work Statement of Architecture Work Re-usable Solution Building Blocks (from organization's Solutions Continuum) Impact Analysis – detailed Implementation Plan and Migration Plan (including Architecture Implementation Contract)	Impact Analysis – Implementation Recommendations Architecture Contract The architecture-compliant implemented system
Phase H: Architecture Change Management (see Chapter 14)	Request for Architecture Change – technology changes Request for Architecture Change – business changes	Architecture updates Changes to architecture framework and principles New Request for Architecture Work, to move to another cycle

3.9 ADM Architecture Requirements Management
(Syllabus reference: 1.R.1)

The process of managing architecture requirements applies to all phases of the ADM cycle, as shown in Figure 3-3.

The Requirements Management process is a dynamic process, which addresses the identification of requirements for the enterprise, storing them and then feeding them in and out of the relevant ADM phases. As shown in Figure 3-3, this process is central to driving the ADM process.

The ability to deal with changes in the requirements is crucial to the ADM process, since architecture by its very nature deals with uncertainty and change, bridging the divide between the aspirations of the stakeholders and what can be delivered as a practical solution.

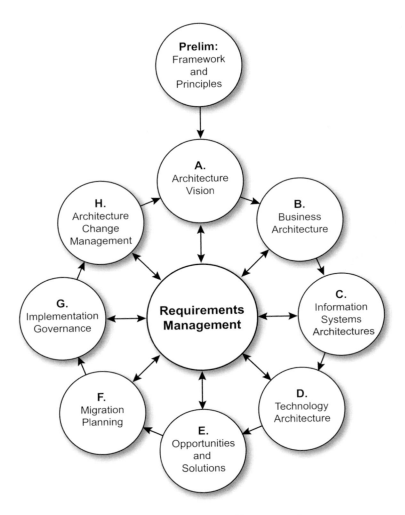

Figure 3.3: ADM Architecture Requirements Management

The Requirements Management process does not itself dispose of, address or prioritize requirements; this is done within the relevant phase of the ADM.

TOGAF does not recommend any specific process or tool for managing requirements, but the Volère web site[1] has a useful list of tools. Business scenarios are appropriate and useful for discovering and documenting business requirements, and for articulating an Architecture Vision (see TOGAF 8.1.1 Enterprise Edition Part IV: Resource Base, Business Scenarios).

---

[1]   Refer to www.volere.co.uk/tools.htm.

Volère Requirements Specification Template

While not designed with architecture requirements in mind, this is a very useful requirements template, which is freely available.

The "Waiting Room"

One interesting item in this template is the "waiting room", which is a holdall for requirements in waiting. There are often requirements identified which, as a result of the prioritization activity that forms part of the Requirements Management process (see below), are designated as beyond the planned scope, or the time available, for the current iteration of the architecture. The waiting room is a repository of future requirements. Having the ability to store such requirements helps avoid the perception that they are simply being discarded, while at the same time helping to manage expectations about what will be delivered.

3.9.1 Inputs

The inputs to the Requirements Management process are the requirements-related outputs from each ADM phase.

The first high-level requirements are produced as part of the Architecture Vision. Each architecture domain then generates detailed requirements. Deliverables in later ADM phases contain mappings to new types of requirements (for example, conformance requirements).

3.9.2 Key Steps

Table 3-4 lists the correspondence between Requirements Management process steps and ADM phase steps.

3.9.3 Outputs

The output from the Requirements Management process is a structured requirements statement, including:

- Changed requirements
- Requirements Impact Statement, which identifies the phases of the ADM that need to be revisited to address any changes. The final version must include the full implications of the requirements (e.g., costs, timescales, and business metrics).

Table 3.4: The Correspondence between Requirements Managements and the ADM Phases

Step	Requirements Management Steps	ADM Phase Steps
1		Identify/document requirements – use business scenarios, or an analogous technique
2	Baseline requirements: 1. Determine priorities arising from current phase of ADM 2. Confirm stakeholder buy-in to resultant priorities 3. Record requirements priorities and place in requirements repository.	
3	Monitor baseline requirements	
4		Identify changed requirement: 1. Remove or re-assess priorities 2. Add requirements and re-assess priorities 3. Modify existing requirements
5	Identify changed requirement and record priorities: 1. Identify changed requirements and ensure the requirements are prioritized by the architect(s) responsible for the current phase, and by the relevant stakeholders 2. Record new priorities 3. Ensure that any conflicts are identified and managed through the phases to a successful conclusion and prioritization 4. Generate Requirements Impact Statement for steering the architecture team **Notes:** 1. Changed requirements can come in through any route. To ensure that the requirements are properly assessed and prioritized, this process needs to direct the ADM phases and record the decisions related to the requirements. 2. The Requirements Management phase needs to determine stakeholder satisfaction with the decisions. Where there is dissatisfaction, the phase remains accountable to ensure the resolution of the issues and determine next steps.	

Step	Requirements Management Steps	ADM Phase Steps
6		1. Assess impact of changed requirements on current (active) phase 2. Assess impact of changed requirements on previous phases 3. Determine whether to implement change, or defer to later ADM cycle; if decision is to implement, assess timescale for change management implementation 4. Issue Requirements Impact Statement,Version n+1
7		Implement requirements arising from Phase H. The architecture can be changed through its lifecycle by the Architecture Change Management phase (Phase H). The Requirements Management process ensures that new or changing requirements that are derived from Phase H are managed accordingly
8	Update the requirements repository with information relating to the changes requested, including stakeholder views affected	
9		Implement change in the current phase
10		Assess and revise gap analysis for past phases The gap analysis in the ADM Phases B through D identifies the gaps between Baseline and Target Architectures; certain types of gap can give rise to gap requirements. The ADM describes two kinds of gap: 1. Something that is present in the baseline, but not in the target (i.e., eliminated – by accident or design) 2. Something not in the baseline, but present in the target (i.e., new) A "gap requirement" is anything that has been eliminated by accident, and therefore requires a change to the Target Architecture. If the gap analysis generates gap requirements, then this step will ensure that they are addressed, documented, and recorded in the requirements repository, and that the Target Architecture is revised accordingly.

3.10 Summary

The TOGAF ADM is a comprehensive general method. It defines a recommended sequence for the various phases and steps involved in developing an architecture. A number of inputs and outputs are recommended for each phase.

The TOGAF ADM is an iterative method. New decisions have to be taken at each iteration of the method:

1. Enterprise coverage
2. Level of detail
3. Time horizon
4. Architecture asset re-use:
   — Previous ADM iterations
   — Other frameworks, system models, industry models, …

Decisions taken should be based on competence and/or resource availability, and the value accruing to the enterprise.

The ADM does not recommend a scope; this has to be determined by the organization itself.

The choice of scope is critical to the success of the architecting effort. The main guideline is to focus on what creates value to the enterprise, and to select horizontal and vertical scope, and project schedules, accordingly. This exercise will be repeated, and future iterations will build on what is being created in the current effort, adding greater width and depth.

Where necessary, use of the ADM should be tailored to meet the needs of the organization. This means that some phases may be omitted, modified, or even additional procedures added.

Requirements Management is an ongoing activity of the ADM. The requirements repository contains the current requirements for the Target Architecture. When new requirements arise, or existing ones are changed, a Requirements Impact Statement is generated, which identifies the phases of the ADM that need to be revisited to address the changes. The statement goes through various iterations until the final version, which includes the full implications of the requirements (e.g., costs, timescales, business metrics) on the architecture development.

3.11 **Test Yourself Questions**

Q1:   TOGAF's ADM is specifically designed to best address:

A.   Business Requirements

B.   Technical Requirements

C.   Social Requirements

D.   Other Requirements

E.   All of these

Q2:   Which of the following statements does not describe the phases of the ADM?

A.   They are cyclical.

B.   They are iterative.

C.   Each phase refines the scope.

D.   Each phase is mandatory.

E.   They cycle through a range of architecture views.

Q3:   Which of the following is not a phase of the ADM?

A.   Preliminary Phase: Framework and Principles

B.   Phase C: Business Architecture

C.   Phase F: Migration and Planning

D.   Phase D: Technology Architecture

E.   Phase G: Implementation Governance

Q4:   Which of these is not a factor to consider when setting the scope of the architecture activity?

A.   The scope or focus of the enterprise

B.   The set of architecture domains to be considered

C.   The level of detail

D.   The time horizon

E.   The Data Architecture

Q5:   Which one of the statements below best completes the following statement? Phase E: Opportunities and Solutions:

A.   Prepares the organization for a successful architecture project

B.   Is used to develop the systems architecture

C.   Identifies the major implementation projects

D.   Produces an implementation roadmap

E.   Ensures that the project conforms to the architecture

Q6:   Which one of the following is an ongoing activity throughout the
      ADM cycle?
      A.   Preliminary Phase
      B.   Requirements Management
      C.   Business Architecture
      D.   Technology Architecture
      E.   Architecture Vision

Q7:   Which of the following is not a resource recommended for
      Requirements Management?
      A.   Business Scenarios
      B.   Gap Analysis
      C.   Volère Requirements Specification template
      D.   Requirements tools
      E.   Volère "waiting room" template

3.12 Recommended Reading

The following are recommended sources of further information for this
chapter:
- TOGAF 8.1.1 Enterprise Edition Part II: ADM, Introduction to the ADM
- TOGAF 8.1.1 Enterprise Edition Part II: ADM, ADM Input and Output
  Descriptions
- TOGAF 8.1.1 Enterprise Edition Part II: ADM, ADM Architecture
  Requirements Management
- TOGAF 8.1.1 Enterprise Edition Part IV: Resource Base, Business
  Scenarios

Chapter 4

Preliminary Phase: Framework and Principles

4.1 Key Learning Points

This chapter describes the Preliminary Phase within the TOGAF
Architecture Development Method (ADM).

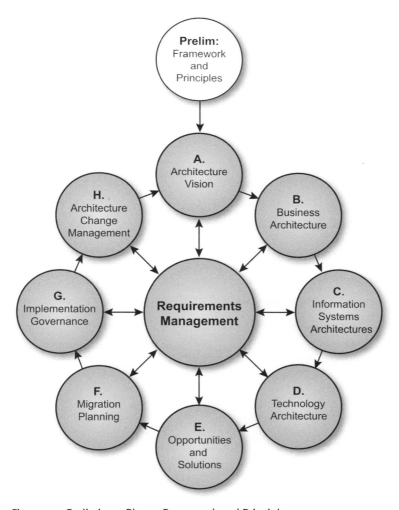

Figure 4.1: Preliminary Phase: Framework and Principles

Key Points Explained

This chapter will help you to answer the following questions:

- What are the objectives of the Preliminary Phase?
- What does the Preliminary Phase consist of?
- What are the inputs needed for the Preliminary Phase?
- What are the outputs from the Preliminary Phase?

4.2 Preliminary Phase: Objectives

The objectives of the Preliminary Phase are as follows:

- To confirm the commitment of the stakeholders
- To define the constraining principles
- To identify an organization's "architecture footprint"; that is, the people responsible for performing the architecture work, where they are located, and their responsibilities
- To define the scope and assumptions; this is particularly important for large organizations where there may be a federated architecture environment
- To define the framework and detailed methodologies that are going to be used to develop the enterprise architecture in the organization; this is typically an adaptation of the ADM
- To set up and monitor the framework's fitness-for-purpose; normally this includes an initial pilot project to check the viability of the approach within the organization
- To define the evaluation criteria for tools, repositories, and management processes to: capture, publish, and maintain architecture artifacts

> TOGAF provides significant guidance on establishing effective architecture governance and coordinating with other governance processes within the organization. Effective governance ensures that problems are identified early and that subsequent changes to the environment occur in a controlled manner.
> *Bill Estrem, "TOGAF to the Rescue"* (www.opengroup.org/downloads)

4.3 Preliminary Phase: Inputs

The Preliminary Phase takes as inputs:

- TOGAF Architecture Development Method (ADM)
- Other architecture framework(s)
- Business strategy (including goals and drivers)
- IT governance strategy
- Architecture principles, including business principles
- Other federated architecture principles

4.4 Preliminary Phase: Steps

The Preliminary Phase consists of two main steps:

1. Defining "How we do Architecture": Principles and Framework
2. Establishing IT Architecture Governance

4.4.1 Step 1: Defining "How we do Architecture"

(Syllabus reference 1.P.1)

Defining how an organization does architecture is the most important goal of the Preliminary Phase. This step has two main aspects: defining the principles and defining the framework.

In large organizations with federated architectures, requirements from a higher-level architecture often appear as "principles" in lower-level ones. This usually takes the form of a principle stating that the lower-level architecture must adhere to the principles of the higher-level architecture. Another example might be a technology principle that has been passed down, such as all network assets must be IPV6-capable.

4.4.1.1 Defining Architecture Principles

(Syllabus reference 1.P.3)

Principles are general rules and guidelines that inform the way in which an organization fulfills its mission. Principles are intended to be enduring and seldom amended. For further information on principles see Section 15.2.2

and TOGAF 8.1.1 Enterprise Edition Part IV: Resource Base, Architecture Principles.

Depending on the organization, principles may be established at any or all of three levels:

- **Enterprise principles** provide a basis for decision-making and dictate how the organization fulfills its mission. Such principles are commonly found in governmental and not-for-profit organizations, but are also found in commercial organizations, as a means of harmonizing decision-making. They are a key element in a successful architecture governance strategy.
- **IT principles** provide guidance on the use and deployment of all IT resources and assets across the enterprise. They are developed to make the information environment as productive and cost-effective as possible.
- **Architecture principles** are a subset of IT principles that relate to architecture work. They reflect a level of consensus across the enterprise, and embody the spirit of the enterprise architecture. Architecture principles can be further divided into:
  — **Principles that govern the architecture process**, affecting the development, maintenance, and use of the enterprise architecture
  — **Principles that govern the implementation of the architecture** (see TOGAF 8.1.1 Enterprise Edition Part IV: Resource Base, Architecture Principles)

TOGAF defines a standard way of describing principles. In addition to a definition statement, each principle should have associated rationale and implications statements, both to promote understanding and acceptance of the principles themselves, and to support the use of the principles in explaining and justifying why specific decisions are made. A recommended template is shown in Table 4-1.

Example 4-1 is a set of principles drawn up in the Preliminary Phase by The Open Group in one of its own architecture projects.[1]

Each of these principles is then expanded into a statement with rationale and implications. Two of these expansions are shown in Example 4-2 and Example 4-3.

---

1 See openshowcase.jotspot.com.

Table 4.1: TOGAF Template for Defining Principles

Name	Should both represent the essence of the rule as well as be easy to remember. Specific technology platforms should not be mentioned in the name or statement of a principle. Avoid ambiguous words in the name and in the statement such as: "support", "open", "consider", and for lack of good measure the word "avoid", itself, be careful with "manage(ment)", and look for unnecessary adjectives and adverbs (fluff).
Statement	Should succinctly and unambiguously communicate the fundamental rule. For the most part, the principles statements for managing information are similar from one organization to the next. It is vital that the principles statement be unambiguous.
Rationale	Should highlight the business benefits of adhering to the principle, using business terminology. Point to the similarity of information and technology principles to the principles governing business operations. Also describe the relationship to other principles, and the intentions regarding a balanced interpretation. Describe situations where one principle would be given precedence or carry more weight than another for making a decision.
Implications	Should highlight the requirements, both for the business and IT, for carrying out the principle – in terms of resources, costs, and activities/tasks. It will often be apparent that current systems, standards, or practices would be incongruent with the principle upon adoption. The impact on the business and consequences of adopting a principle should be clearly stated. The reader should readily discern the answer to: "How does this affect me?" It is important not to oversimplify, trivialize, or judge the merit of the impact. Some of the implications will be identified as potential impacts only, and may be speculative rather than fully analyzed.
Technology Architecture	This describes the logical software and hardware capabilities that are required to support the deployment of business, data, and application services. This includes IT infrastructure, middleware, networks, communications, processing, and standards.

4.4.1.2   Defining the Framework to be Used – Adapting the ADM
(Syllabus reference 1.P.2)

The next part of this step is to define the framework for the architecture development. The outcome could be a statement that the TOGAF ADM is to be used as-is, or a more complex description of an adaptation of the ADM.

Example 4.1: Preliminary Phase Principles

An Example Statement of Principles

Principles guide us in developing the architecture. They should neither undermine each other nor behave as a blockage to the achievement of others. Policies direct execution. We are unlikely to achieve the principles all of the time – but should aspire to get there. The following set of principles have been approved by the Internal Architecture Board:

Business Principles
1. Primacy of Principles
2. Maximize Benefit to the Enterprise
3. Compliance with Law
4. Availability at Anytime from Anywhere
5. Business Continuity
6. Citizenship
7. Custodianship
8. De-Customization
9. Painless User Experience
10. Self-Serve
11. Sharing of Information

Architecture Principles
1. De-Skill
2. One Source
3. Content Management

Example 4.2: Sample Principle 1

Primacy of Principles	
Statement	Principles apply throughout the enterprise and override all other considerations when decisions are made.
Rationale	The only way we can provide a recognized, consistent, and measurable level of operations is if all parts of the enterprise abide by the principles when making decisions.
Implications	Without this principle, short-term consideration, supposedly convenient exceptions, and inconsistencies would rapidly undermine the management of information. Information management initiatives will not be permitted to begin until they are examined for compliance with the principles. A conflict with a principle will be resolved by changing the conflicting initiative, which could delay or prevent the initiative.

Example 4.3: Sample Principle 2

Self-Serve	
Statement	Customers should be able to serve themselves.
Rationale	Applying this principle will improve customer satisfaction, reduce administrative overhead, and potentially improve revenue.
Implications	There is an implication to improve ease-of-use and minimize training needs; for example, members should be able to update their contact details, etc. and be able to buy additional membership products online.

Why is it necessary to consider adapting the ADM?

The ADM is a generic method for architecture development and is designed to deal with most system and organizational requirements. It is sometimes necessary to adapt the ADM because:

- The order of the phases is partly dependent on the maturity of the architecture discipline within the enterprise.
- The order may be defined by the business and architecture principles of an enterprise.
- TOGAF may be integrated with another enterprise framework such as the Zachman Framework.
- The ADM is one of the many corporate processes that make up the corporate governance model.
- The ADM is to be used as a method for something other than enterprise architecture, such as a general program management method.
- The ADM is being mandated for use by a lead contractor in an outsourcing situation, and needs to be tailored to achieve a suitable compromise between the contractor and the contracting enterprise.
- The enterprise is a small-to-medium enterprise, and wishes to use a "cut-down" method.
- The enterprise is very large and complex, which may imply some or all of the following:
  - **Top-down planning and development** – designing the whole meta-enterprise as a single entity (this may stretch the limits of practicality)
  - **Development of a "generic" architecture**, typical of the enterprises within the organization, but not representing any specific enterprise, which individual enterprises are then expected to adapt in order to

produce an architecture "instance" (often referred to as a "Product Line Architecture") suited to the particular enterprise concerned

— **Replication** – developing a specific architecture for one enterprise, implementing it as a proof-of-concept, and then cloning that in other enterprises

If the ADM is being adapted or parts omitted, it is important to document explicitly the rationale for the adaptations or omissions. The recommended approach when omitting steps, phases, and processes from the ADM is to use the principle of positive omission.

Example 4-4 shows a positioning statement for a project that will follow the ADM with minimal adaptation. In this project it is proposed that redundant steps can be omitted with justification.

Example 4.4: Defining how we do Architecture

> **An Example Positioning Statement**
> This architecture development will fully follow all the phases and steps of the Architecture Development Method (ADM) of The Open Group Architecture Framework (TOGAF). Should the scope and size of this development mean that a particular step would be redundant, then that fact will be logged together with the justification for the omission. Whenever it is possible, processes and techniques from the TOGAF Resource Base will be employed.
> Should any inconsistencies in TOGAF be identified, these will be logged and reported to The Open Group Architecture Forum, together with a description of the work-around used in order to resolve the inconsistency.

4.4.2 Step 2: Establishing IT Architecture Governance
(Syllabus reference 1.P.4)

An enterprise architecture is only as good as the decision-making framework that is established around it. This is known as a "governance" framework.

IT governance provides the framework and structure that links IT resources and information to enterprise goals and strategies. It institutionalizes best practices for planning, acquiring, implementing, and monitoring IT performance so that the enterprise's IT assets support its business objectives.

The management of IT-related risk is widely accepted as a key part of enterprise governance. Successful governance depends on establishment of a clear authority structure and the right participants. It follows that an IT governance strategy and an appropriate way to implement it must be established in this phase with the backing of top management, clarifying who owns the enterprise's IT resources, and who has ultimate responsibility for their enterprise-wide integration.

In TOGAF, the body established to oversee governance is referred to as the Architecture Board (see TOGAF 8.1.1 Enterprise Edition Part IV: Resource Base, Architecture Board). An Architecture Board should be representative of all the key stakeholders in the architecture, and typically comprises a group of executives responsible for the review and maintenance of the overall architecture; see Section 15.2.4 and Section 22.2.

4.5 Preliminary Phase: Outputs

The outputs of this phase include the following:

- Architecture principles
- Framework definition
- Restatement of business principles, goals, and drivers

4.6 Summary

The objective of the Preliminary Phase is to prepare an organization for a successful enterprise architecture project by defining "how we do architecture". The steps to doing this are as follows:

- Understanding the business environment
- Obtaining high-level management commitment
- Obtaining agreement on scope
- Establishing architecture principles
- Establishing IT architecture governance structure
- Agreeing the architecture method to be adopted

The outputs should be an initial set of architecture principles, a statement of the architecture methodology adopted, and a restatement of the business principles, goals, and drivers.

4.7 Test Yourself Questions

Q1:   Which one of the following is completed during the Preliminary Phase
       of the TOGAF ADM?
       A.   Architecture Principles
       B.   Gap Analysis
       C.   Impact Analysis
       D.   Statement of Architecture Work
       E.   Requirements Gathering

Q2:   Which one of the following is not an objective of the Preliminary
       Phase?
       A.   Ensuring that everyone who will be involved is committed to the
             project's success
       B.   Identifying the people responsible for performing the architecture
             work, where they are located, and their responsibilities
       C.   Defining the scope of the work and assumptions
       D.   Defining the framework and detailed methodologies
       E.   Developing the Target Business Architecture

Q3:   Which of the following is a reason to adapt the ADM?
       A.   All of the answers below.
       B.   The use of TOGAF is being integrated with another framework.
       C.   The ADM is being used for a purpose other than enterprise
             architecture.
       D.   The enterprise is a large federated organization.
       E.   The IT governance model needs to be tailored.

Q4:   Which of the following statements does not apply to principles?
       A.   A principle is a general rule or guideline.
       B.   A principle is transient and updated frequently.
       C.   An IT principle provides guidance on use and deployment of IT
             resources.
       D.   TOGAF defines a standard way of describing a principle.
       E.   A principle statement should be succinct and unambiguous.

Q5:   Which of the following statements is false? An Architecture Board:
       A.   Is established to oversee governance of the enterprise architecture
       B.   Is responsible for the production of usable governance material

C. Should meet regularly

D. Has a recommended size of 12 members

E. Should represent key stakeholders in the architecture

Q6: Which of the following statements about architecture principles is not true?

A. Principles are general rules and guidelines that inform and support the way in which an organization sets about fulfilling its mission.

B. Principles may be established at any or all of three levels: Enterprise, Information Technology, and Architecture.

C. A set of principles should be Understandable, Robust, Complete, Consistent, and Stable.

D. The principle of Data Security implies that security needs must be identified and developed at the application level.

E. The principle of Technology Independence implies the use of standards which support portability.

4.8 Recommended Reading

The following are recommended sources of further information for this chapter:

- TOGAF 8.1.1 Enterprise Edition Part II: |Introduction to the ADM
- TOGAF 8.1.1 Enterprise Edition Part II: ADM, Preliminary Phase
- TOGAF 8.1.1 Enterprise Edition Part IV: Resource Base, Architecture Board
- TOGAF 8.1.1 Enterprise Edition Part IV: Resource Base, Architecture Principles
- TOGAF 8.1.1 Enterprise Edition Part IV: Resource Base, Architecture Governance

Chapter 5

Phase A: Architecture Vision

5.1 Key Learning Points

This chapter describes Phase A: Architecture Vision of the TOGAF Architecture Development Method (ADM).

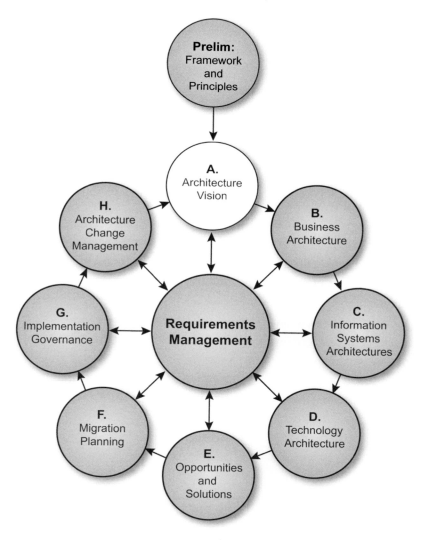

Figure 5.1: Phase A: Architecture Vision

Key Points Explained

This chapter will help you to answer the following questions:

- What are the objectives of the Phase A?
- What does Phase A comprise of?
- What is its relationship to the rest of the TOGAF ADM?
- What are the inputs needed for Phase A?
- What are the outputs from Phase A?

5.2 Objectives

The objectives of Phase A: Architecture Vision are as follows:

- Obtain management commitment for this particular cycle of the ADM
- Validate business principles, goals, and drivers
- Define, scope, and prioritize architecture tasks
- Identify stakeholders, their concerns, and objectives
- Define business requirements and constraints
- Describe appropriate solutions
- Obtain formal approval to proceed
- Understand the influence on, and from, parallel architecture developments

5.3 Inputs

The inputs to this phase are:

- Request for Architecture Work (see Section 15.2.5)
- Business strategy, business goals, and business drivers (see Section 15.2.3)
- Architecture principles (see Section 4.4.1.1 and Section 15.2.2), including business principles
- Enterprise Continuum (see Chapter 18); that is, existing architecture documentation (framework description, architecture descriptions, existing baseline descriptions, etc.)

5.4 Steps

There are seven steps in this phase.

5.4.1 Project Establishment
(Syllabus reference 1.A.1)

In this step you must conduct the necessary procedures to obtain recognition of the project, endorsement by corporate management, and the support and commitment of line management. Reference must be made to the IT governance framework (see Section 15.2.4 and Section 22.2) and an explanation provided of how this project relates to that framework.

5.4.2 Identify Business Goals and Business Drivers
(Syllabus reference 1.A.2)

Here you must identify business goals and strategic drivers of the organization. If these have already been defined elsewhere, ensure that the existing definitions are current and clarify any areas of ambiguity. Otherwise, go back to the originators of the Statement of Architecture Work, define these items again, and get their endorsement by management.

See also Section 15.2.3.

5.4.3 Review Architecture Principles, including Business Principles
(Syllabus reference 1.A.3)

In this step you should review the principles, developed in the Preliminary Phase, under which the architecture is to be developed. Architecture principles are usually based on the business principles developed in the Preliminary Phase. Ensure the existing definitions are current, and clarify any areas of ambiguity.

5.4.4 Define the Scope
(Syllabus reference 1.A.4)

Here you must define the scope of the architecture work (see TOGAF 8.1.1, Part I: Scope of the Architecting Activity, Introduction to the ADM). In particular, define:
- Breadth of coverage
- Level of detail

- The specific architecture domains to be covered (Business, Data, Applications, Technology)
- Schedule the project milestones, including intermediate milestones (termed by TOGAF as the extent of the time horizon)
- The architecture assets to be leveraged from the organization's Enterprise Architecture Continuum
- Assets created in previous iterations of the ADM cycle
- Assets available elsewhere in industry (other frameworks, systems models, vertical industry models, etc.)

5.4.5 Define Constraints
(Syllabus reference 1.A.5)

Define any constraints, including those that are enterprise-wide or project-specific. The former may be influenced by the business and architecture principles developed in the Preliminary Phase. There might be additional technical constraints; for example, mandating use of a particular operating system platform or networking technology.

5.4.6 Identify Stakeholders and Concerns, Business Requirements, and Architecture Vision
(Syllabus reference 1.A.6)

In this step you must identify key stakeholders and their concerns; define key business requirements and articulate an Architecture Vision to address them, within the scope and constraints, whilst conforming to business and architecture principles.

Business scenarios are an appropriate technique to discover and document business requirements, and to produce an Architecture Vision (see below).

This step will generate the first, very high-level definitions of the baseline and target environments, from a business information systems and technology perspective:
- Baseline Business Architecture, Version 0.1
- Baseline Technology Architecture, Version 0.1
- Baseline Data Architecture, Version 0.1
- Baseline Applications Architecture, Version 0.1

- Target Business Architecture, Version 0.1
- Target Technology Architecture, Version 0.1
- Target Data Architecture, Version 0.1
- Target Applications Architecture, Version 0.1

Business Scenarios

The ADM has its own method (a "method-within-a-method") for identifying and articulating the business requirements implied in new business functionality to address key business drivers, and the implied Technology Architecture requirements. This process is known as "business scenarios".

A business scenario is a description of a business problem, which enables requirements to be viewed in relation to one another in the context of the overall problem. Without such a description to serve as context, the business value of solving the problem is unclear, the relevance of potential solutions is unclear, and there is a danger of the solution being based on an inadequate set of requirements.

A key factor in the success of any other major project is the extent to which it is linked to business requirements, and demonstrably supports and enables the enterprise to achieve its business objectives. Business scenarios are an important technique to help identify and understand business needs.

The technique may be used iteratively, at different levels of detail in the hierarchical decomposition of the Business Architecture. The generic business scenario process is as follows:

- Identify, document, and rank the problem that is driving the project
- Document, as high-level architecture models, the business and technical environments where the problem situation is occurring
- Identify and document desired objectives; the results of handling the problems successfully
- Identify human actors and their place in the business model, the human participants, and their roles
- Identify computer actors and their place in the technology model, the computing elements, and their roles
- Identify and document roles, responsibilities, and measures of success per actor, the required scripts per actor, and the desired results of handling the situation properly
- Check for fitness-for-purpose of inspiring subsequent architecture work, and refine only if necessary

> The business scenario process is covered in depth in TOGAF 8.1.1 Part IV: Resource
> Base. The Open Group also publishes a Guide to Business Scenarios as part of its
> Manager's Guide series (G261), together with a number of actual scenarios in its
> online bookstore, available at www.opengroup.org/bookstore.

5.4.7 Document the Statement of Architecture Work and Gain Approval
(Syllabus reference 1.A.7)

The Statement of Architecture Work should be produced (see Section
15.2.6 for a description of the contents of this deliverable). Approval of this
document by the governing body (usually the Architecture Board) should be
sought.

5.5 Outputs
The outputs of this phase include the following:
- Approved Statement of Architecture Work including:
  — Scope and constraint
  — Plan for the architecture work
- Refined statements of business goals and strategic drivers
- Architecture principles, including business principles
- Architecture Vision (produced by the business scenario) including:
  — Baseline Business Architecture, Version 0.1
  — Baseline Technology Architecture, Version 0.1
  — Baseline Data Architecture, Version 0.1
  — Baseline Applications Architecture, Version 0.1
  — Target Business Architecture, Version 0.1
  — Target Technology Architecture, Version 0.1
  — Target Data Architecture, Version 0.1
  — Target Applications Architecture, Version 0.1

5.6 Summary
Phase A: Architecture Vision is about project establishment and initiates
an iteration of the architecture process. It sets the scope, constraints, and
expectations for this iteration of the ADM. It is required at the start of every
architecture cycle, in order to validate the business context and create the
Statement of Architecture Work.

5.7 Test Yourself Questions

Q1:   Complete the following sentence: Phase A: Architecture Vision of the TOGAF ADM is initiated upon receipt of a(n):
  A.   Approval from the Chief Information Officer
  B.   Requirements Analysis
  C.   Implementation Plan
  D.   Directive from the Chief Executive Officer
  E.   Request for Architecture Work from the sponsoring organization

Q2:   Which of the following is not a direct input to Phase A: Architecture Vision?
  A.   Request for Architecture Work
  B.   Impact Analysis
  C.   Architecture Principles
  D.   Existing architecture documentation
  E.   Existing Baseline Architecture descriptions

Q3:   Complete the following sentence: Phase A: Architecture Vision is intended to do all of the following except:
  A.   Validate the business principles and goals of the organization
  B.   Ensure that the architecture principles are correct
  C.   Establish IT governance
  D.   Clarify and correct ambiguities in the architecture principles
  E.   Define the specific architecture domains to be addressed

Q4:   What is an appropriate technique to document business requirements in Phase A: Architecture Vision?
  A.   Business Architecture Report
  B.   Gap Analysis
  C.   Business Principles
  D.   Business Scenarios
  E.   Impact Analysis

Q5:   Which of the following best describes the output from Phase A: Architecture Vision?
  A.   Approved Statement of Architecture Work
  B.   Plan for the Architecture Work
  C.   Baseline Business Architecture, Version 0.1

D.   Architecture Principles

E.   All of these

Q6:   The Architecture Vision is the architect's key opportunity to sell the benefits of the proposed developments to the decision-makers. Which of the following does TOGAF describe this as?

A.   The baseline

B.   The elevator pitch

C.   The 10,000 foot view

D.   The visionary view

E.   All of these

Q7:   Which of the following statements about the scope of the architecture effort is not true?

A.   Scope includes the level of detail to be defined.

B.   Scope includes the specific architecture domains to be covered (Business, Data, Applications, Technology).

C.   Scope does not include the extent of the time horizon.

D.   Scope includes assets created in previous iterations of the ADM cycle.

E.   Scope includes assets available elsewhere in the industry.

5.8 Recommended Reading

The following are recommended sources of further information for this chapter:

- TOGAF 8.1.1 Enterprise Edition Part II: ADM, Introduction to the ADM
- TOGAF 8.1.1 Enterprise Edition Part II: ADM, Phase A: Architecture Vision
- TOGAF 8.1.1 Enterprise Edition Part II: ADM, ADM Input and Output Descriptions
- TOGAF 8.1.1 Enterprise Edition Part IV: Resource Base, Architecture Principles
- TOGAF 8.1.1 Enterprise Edition Part IV: Resource Base, Business Scenarios

Chapter 6

Phase B: Business Architecture

6.1 Key Learning Points

This chapter describes Phase B: Business Architecture of the TOGAF
Architecture Development Method (ADM).

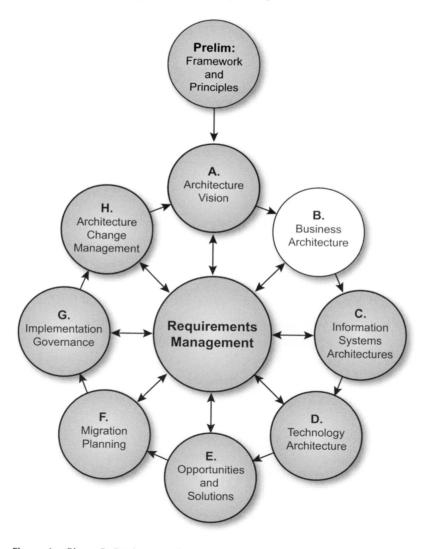

Figure 6.1: Phase B: Business Architecture

Key Points Explained

This chapter will help you to answer the following questions:

- What are the objectives of the Phase B?
- What does Phase B consist of?
- What is its relationship to the rest of the TOGAF ADM?
- What are the inputs needed for Phase B?
- What are the outputs from Phase B?

6.2 Objectives

The objectives of Phase B: Business Architecture are as follows:

- Select architecture viewpoints to demonstrate how stakeholder concerns are addressed in the Business Architecture
- Select tools and techniques for viewpoints
- Describe the existing Business Architecture (the current baseline)
- Develop a Target Business Architecture
- Analyze the gaps between the Baseline and Target Architectures

6.3 Introduction

Knowledge of the Business Architecture is a prerequisite for architecture work in other domains (Data, Applications, Technology), and so is the first activity that needs to be undertaken.

The Business Architecture is often necessary for demonstrating the business value of subsequent work to key stakeholders, and their return on investment. The business scenario technique of the TOGAF ADM is an appropriate method for eliciting business requirements. A key objective is to re-use existing material. In some cases there will be architecture definitions that can be used as a starting point (see Chapter 19).

The extent of the work in this phase will depend on the enterprise environment. In some cases, key elements of the Business Architecture may be done in other activities. In such cases, there may be a need to verify and update the current business strategy and plans, and/or to bridge between high-level business drivers, business strategy, and goals on the one hand, and the specific business requirements on the other. (The business strategy typically defines goals, drivers, and metrics for success but not how to get there; that is role of the Business Architecture.)

In other cases, little or no Business Architecture work may have been done. In such cases, the architecture team must research, verify, and gain buy-in to the key business objectives and processes that the architecture is to support. This may be done as a freestanding exercise, either preceding architecture development, or as part of Phase A: Architecture Vision.

6.4 Inputs

The inputs to this phase are:

- Request for Architecture Work (see Section 15.2)
- Approved Statement of Architecture Work (see Section 15.2.6)
- Refined statements of business goals and strategic drivers
- Architecture principles (see Section 4.4.1.1 and Section 15.2.2), including business principles
- Enterprise Continuum (as described in Chapter 18)
- Architecture Vision (see Section 15.2.7), including:
  — Baseline Business Architecture, Version 0.1
  — Baseline Technology Architecture, Version 0.1
  — Baseline Data Architecture, Version 0.1
  — Baseline Applications Architecture, Version 0.1
  — Target Business Architecture, Version 0.1
  — Target Technology Architecture, Version 0.1
  — Target Data Architecture, Version 0.1
  — Target Applications Architecture, Version 0.1

6.5 Steps

The eight key steps in this phase are outlined below.

The order of the steps should be adapted to the situation: in particular, you should determine whether it is appropriate to do the Baseline Business Architecture or the Target Business Architecture development first.

6.5.1 Develop Baseline Business Architecture Description
(Syllabus reference 1.B.1)

Develop a Baseline Description of the existing Business Architecture. This analysis is usually done bottom-up. The scope and level of detail depends on the extent to which existing business elements are carried over into the Target Business Architecture, and on whether any architecture descriptions exist. Identify the relevant Business Architecture Building Blocks, drawing on the Architecture Continuum.

Building Blocks

Building blocks are used widely within TOGAF for building architectures, where they are known as Architecture Building Blocks (ABBs) and for building solutions, where they are known as Solution Building Blocks (SBBs).

A building block is simply a package of functionality defined to meet business needs. Examples of ABBs for an online store might include an order processing building block, a customer information system building block, a product inventory building block, etc. Equivalent SBBs would be products that implement the functionality required.

Building blocks have generic characteristics as follows:

- A building block is a package of functionality defined to meet the business needs across an organization. For example, an organization might have an overall Business Architecture model with a payment handling building block within that.
- A building block has published interfaces to access the functionality.
- A building block may interoperate with other, inter-dependent building blocks.

A good building block has the following characteristics:

- It considers implementation and usage, and evolves to exploit technology and standards.
- It may be assembled from other building blocks.
- It may be a subassembly of other building blocks.
- Ideally, a building block is re-usable and replaceable, and well specified.

A building block may have multiple implementations but with different inter-dependent building blocks.

The way in which functionality, products, and custom developments are assembled into building blocks varies widely between individual architectures. Every organization must decide for itself what arrangement of building blocks works best for it. A good choice of building blocks can lead to improvements in legacy system integration, interoperability, and flexibility in the creation of new systems and applications.

Systems are built up from collections of building blocks, so most building blocks have to interoperate with other building blocks. Wherever that is true, it is important that the interfaces to a building block are published and reasonably stable.

See also Section 15.2.21 and Section 15.2.22.

6.5.2   Identify Reference Models, Viewpoints, and Tools
(Syllabus reference 1.B.2)

Architecture Views and Viewpoints

Two terms are used extensively in TOGAF when describing the architecture: view and viewpoint.

A **view** is a representation of a whole system from the perspective of a related set of concerns.

A **viewpoint** defines the perspective from which a view is taken.

When modeling a system you should identify a viewpoint for each different stakeholder. Then identify a related set of concerns associated with a viewpoint, known as the view. Views of different stakeholders can overlap.

See Section 15.2.19 and Section 15.2.20 for key definitions related to architecture views and an example.

1. Select relevant Business Architecture resources (reference models, patterns, etc.) from the Architecture Continuum.
2. Select relevant Business Architecture viewpoints (e.g., Operations, Management, Financial). These will enable the architect to demonstrate how stakeholder concerns are being addressed.
3. Identify appropriate tools and techniques to be used for capture, modeling, and analysis in association with the viewpoints. These may comprise simple documents or more sophisticated modeling tools and techniques such as activity models, business process models, use-case models, etc.

6.5.3 Create Business Architecture Model(s)

(Syllabus reference 1.B.3)

1. For each viewpoint, create the model for the specific view required, using the selected tool or method.
2. Ensure that all stakeholder concerns are covered. If they are not, create new models or augment existing models. The business scenarios process (see Section 5.4.6) can be used for discovering and documenting business requirements in this phase. Other techniques may also be used. Create models of the following:
   a. **Organization structure** identifying business locations and relating them to organizational units
   b. **Business goals and objectives** for each organizational unit
   c. **Business functions**; this is a recursive step involving successive decomposition of major functional areas into sub-functions
   d. **Business services** that each of the enterprise units provides to its customers, both internally and externally
   e. **Business processes**, including measures and deliverables
   f. **Business roles**, including development and modification of skills requirements
   g. **Correlation of organization and functions** in the form of a matrix report
3. **Information requirements**: identify for each business function: when, where, how often, and by whom the function is performed, what information is used, and its source(s), and what opportunities exist for improvements; include information that needs to be created or modified
4. **Perform trade-off analysis** to resolve conflicts among the different views using, for example, CMU/SEI's Architecture Trade-off Analysis Method (ATAM)
5. Validate that the models support the principles, objectives, and constraints
6. Note changes to the viewpoint represented in the selected models from the Architecture Continuum and document them
7. Test architecture models for completeness against requirements

Architecture Trade-off Analysis Method (ATAM)

Developed by the Software Engineering Institute at the Carnegie Mellon University, ATAM is a method for software architecture evaluation. Its purpose is to help choose a suitable architecture for a software system by discovering trade-offs and sensitivity points.

For more information go to www.sei.cmu.edu/architecture/ata_method.html.

6.5.4 Select Business Architecture Building Blocks
(Syllabus reference 1.B.4)
1. Identify required building blocks and check against the library of building blocks, re-using as appropriate
2. Where necessary, define new Business Architecture Building Blocks

See also Section 15.2.21.

6.5.5 Conduct a Formal Checkpoint Review of the Architecture Model and Building Blocks with Stakeholders
(Syllabus reference 1.B.5)

This is a formal review of the model and building blocks selected in the earlier steps of this phase. The purpose is to compare the proposed Business Architecture against the Statement of Architecture Work. This is a point where you can loop back to earlier steps if the review indicates it is required.

6.5.6 Review Non-Functional (Qualitative) Criteria
(Syllabus reference 1.B.6)

This review of non-functional (qualitative) criteria (e.g., performance, cost) is used to specify required service levels and can lead to the generation of formal Service Level Agreements (SLAs).

6.5.7 Complete the Business Architecture
(Syllabus reference 1.B.7)
1. Select standards for each of the Architecture Building Blocks, re-using where possible from the Architecture Continuum
2. Fully document each Architecture Building Block
3. Cross-check the overall architecture against the business requirements

4. Document final requirements traceability report
5. Document final mapping of the architecture within the Architecture Continuum. From the selected Architecture Building Blocks, identify those that might be re-used and publish via the architecture repository
6. Document the rationale for all building block decisions in the architecture document
7. Prepare a Business Architecture Report (a log of the activity in this phase). Generate the Business Architecture document (see Section 15.2.9)
8. Checkpoint: Check the original motivation for the architecture project and the Statement of Architecture Work against the proposed Business Architecture; conduct an Impact Analysis, to determine if it is fit-for-purpose and, if necessary, rework

Gap Analysis

The technique known as gap analysis is widely used in the TOGAF ADM to validate an architecture that is being developed. The technique involves drawing up a matrix to highlight any shortfalls between a Baseline Architecture and a Target Architecture.

See Section 15.2.12 for full details of the gap analysis technique including an example.

6.5.8 Perform Gap Analysis and Create Report
(Syllabus reference 1.B.8)

At this point a gap analysis should be undertaken and a report generated. This is a key step in validating that the architecture supports all of the essential information processing needs of the organization. Gaps may be found by considering stakeholders' concerns. Other potential sources include:

• People (e.g., cross-training requirements)
• Processes
• Tools
• Information
• Measurement
• Financial
• Facilities (buildings, office space, etc.)

Gap analysis highlights services and/or functions that have been omitted or are yet to be developed or procured; these are known as "gaps". They should either then be explained as correctly eliminated or marked to be addressed by reinstating, developing, or procuring the functionality. See Section 15.2.12 for full details of the gap analysis technique.

6.6 Outputs

The outputs of this phase include the following:

- Statement of Architecture Work, updated if necessary
- Validated business principles, business goals, and strategic drivers
- Target Business Architecture, Version 1.0 (detailed), including:
  — Organization structure – identifying business locations and relating them to organizational units
  — Business goals and objectives, for the enterprise and each organizational unit
  — Business functions – a detailed, recursive step involving successive decomposition of major functional areas into sub-functions
  — Business services – the services that the enterprise and each enterprise unit provides to its customers, both internally and externally
  — Business processes, including measures and deliverables
  — Business roles, including development and modification of skills requirements
  — Business data model
  — Correlation of organization and functions – relate business functions to organizational units in the form of a matrix report
- Baseline Business Architecture, Version 1.0 (detailed)
- Views corresponding to the selected viewpoints addressing key stakeholder concerns
- Gap analysis results
- Technical requirements identifying, categorizing, and prioritizing the implications for work in the remaining architecture domains (for example, by a dependency/priority matrix); list the specific models that are expected to be produced (for example, expressed as primitives of the Zachman Framework)
- Business Architecture Report
- Updated business requirements

6.7 Summary

The objective of Phase B: Business Architecture is to document the fundamental organization of a business, embodied in its business processes and people, their relationships to each other and the environment, and the principles governing its design and evolution. It should show how the organization meets its business goals.

The description of the business should address the following:
- Organization structure
- Business goals and objectives
- Business functions
- Business services
- Business processes
- Business roles
- Correlation of organization and functions

The steps in this phase are as follows:
- Confirm context
- Define the Baseline Description of the existing Business Architecture
- Define a Target Business Architecture:
  — For each viewpoint, create the model for the specific view required
- Validate:
  — Requirements
  — Concerns
- Gap analysis
- Produce report

6.8 Test Yourself Questions

Q1: Business Architecture is the first architecture activity undertaken since:

A. It is often necessary to demonstrate the business value of the overall architecture activity.

B. It provides knowledge that is a prerequisite for undertaking architecture work in the other domains (Data, Applications, Technology).

C. It can be used to demonstrate the return on investment to key stakeholders.

D. It embodies the fundamental organization of a business and shows how an organization meets its business goals.

E. All of these

Q2: TOGAF suggests, but does not require the use of <...> to analyze business requirements.

A. Gap Analysis

B. Business Scenarios

C. SWOT Analysis

D. Fishbone Diagrams

E. Mind Maps

Q3: Architecture views:

A. Are representations of the overall architecture that are meaningful to one or more stakeholders

B. Provide an assessment of the skills required to deliver successful enterprise architecture

C. Are aimed at speeding the process of developing applications

D. Are sets of owned responsibilities that ensure integrity of the organization's architecture

E. Are detailed design requirements specific to a phase of the ADM

Q4: Which of the following is not an appropriate tool or technique for capture, modeling, and analysis in association with the viewpoints?

A. Activity Models

B. Class Models

C. Use-case Models

D. UML Business Class Models

E. Resource-Event-Agent business models

Q5: Gap analysis is a key step in validating the architecture in Phase B: Business Architecture. Which of the following statements is true?

A. Gap analysis highlights services that are available.

B. Gap analysis highlights the impacts of change.

C. Gap analysis highlights services that are yet to be procured.

D. Gap analysis identifies areas where the Data Architecture needs to change.

E. Gap analysis can be used to resolve conflicts amongst different viewpoints.

6.9 Recommended Reading

The following are recommended sources of further information for this chapter:

- TOGAF 8.1.1 Enterprise Edition Part II: ADM, Phase B: Business Architecture
- TOGAF 8.1.1 Enterprise Edition Part II: ADM, ADM Input and Output Descriptions
- TOGAF 8.1.1 Enterprise Edition Part IV: Resource Base, Developing Architecture Views
- TOGAF 8.1.1 Enterprise Edition Part IV: Resource Base, Building Blocks
- TOGAF 8.1.1 Enterprise Edition Part IV: Resource Base, Business Scenarios

Chapter 7

Phase C: Information Systems Architectures

7.1 Key Learning Points

This chapter gives a high-level overview of Phase C: Information Systems Architectures of the TOGAF Architecture Development Method (ADM). Further details are provided in Chapter 8 and Chapter 9.

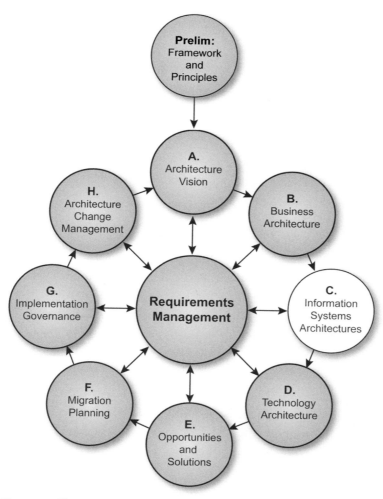

Figure 7.1: Phase C: Information Systems Architectures

Key Points Explained

This chapter will help you to answer the following questions:

- What are the objectives of the Phase C?
- What does Phase C consist of?
- What is its relationship to the rest of the TOGAF ADM?
- What are the inputs needed for Phase C?
- What are the outputs from Phase C?

7.2 Objectives

The objective of Phase C is to develop Target Architectures for the Data and/ or the Applications domains. The scope of the business processes supported in this phase is limited to those that are supported by IT and the interfaces of those IT-related processes to non-IT-related processes.

7.3 Approach

Phase C involves some combination of Data and Applications Architecture. These may be developed in either order, or in parallel. Theory suggests Data Architecture comes first, but practical considerations may mean that starting with application systems may be more efficient. There will need to be some iteration to ensure consistency.

One common approach is top-down design and bottom-up implementation. This means that the design starts with Business Architecture, and then progresses to Data (or Applications) Architecture, then Applications (or Data) Architecture before finally designing the Technology Architecture. Implementation then reverses this, starting with Technology Architecture before implementing the Applications (or Data) Architecture, then the Data (or Applications) Architecture and finally the Business Architecture. This makes sense since you need the Technology Architecture to be implemented first to allow the other architectures to build upon it. An alternative approach is a data-driven sequence, such as recommended in Steven Spewak's Enterprise Architecture Planning (EAP), whereby application systems that create data are implemented first, then those that process it, and finally applications that archive it.

7.4 Inputs

The inputs to this phase are:

- Application principles
- Data principles
- Request for Architecture Work
- Statement of Architecture Work
- Architecture Vision
- Enterprise Continuum (see Chapter 18)
- Baseline Business Architecture, Version 1.0 (detailed)
- Target Business Architecture, Version 1.0 (detailed)
- Baseline Data Architecture, Version 0.1
- Target Data Architecture, Version 0.1
- Baseline Applications Architecture, Version 0.1
- Target Applications Architecture Version 0.1
- Relevant technical requirements that will apply to Phase C
- Gap analysis results (from Business Architecture)
- Re-usable building blocks (from organization's Architecture Continuum)

7.5 Steps

There are two steps in this phase:

1. Data Architecture
2. Applications Architecture

The details for these are covered in the following two chapters.

7.6 Outputs

The outputs of this phase include the following:

- Statement of Architecture Work
- Baseline Data Architecture, Version 1.0
- Target Data Architecture, Version 1.0
- Baseline Applications Architecture, Version 1.0
- Target Applications Architecture, Version 1.0
- Data Architecture views corresponding to the selected viewpoints addressing key stakeholder concerns
- Applications Architecture views corresponding to the selected viewpoints addressing key stakeholder concerns

- Data Architecture Report, summarizing what was done and the key findings
- Applications Architecture Report, summarizing what was done and the key findings
- Gap analysis results:
  — Areas where the Business Architecture may need to change to cater for changes in the Data and/or Applications Architecture
  — Constraints on the Technology Architecture about to be designed
- Impact Analysis
- Updated business requirements

7.7 Summary

The objective of Phase C: Information Systems Architectures is to document the fundamental organization of an organization's IT system, embodied in the major types of information and the application systems that process them, their relationships to each other and the environment, and the principles governing its design and evolution. It should document how the IT systems meet the business goals of the enterprise.

7.8 Test Yourself Questions

Q1:   Which of the following is the objective of Phase C: Information Systems Architectures?

    A.   Developing the Target Business Architecture

    B.   Developing the Target Data and Applications Architectures

    C.   Developing the Target Technology Architecture

    D.   Evaluating the Target Architectures

    E.   Developing an applications and data Migration Plan

Q2:   TOGAF recommends which of the following steps be completed in Phase C?

    A.   Data Architecture first

    B.   Applications Architecture first

    C.   Either Data Architecture or Applications Architecture, as long as they are in sequence

    D.   Data Architecture and Applications Architecture must be carried out in parallel

E. Either Data Architecture or Applications Architecture first, or both in parallel, depending on the project scope and best fit with the Business Architecture

Q3: Which of the following statements about Phase C is true?
A. A common implementation approach is bottom-up design and top-down implementation.
B. The Data Architecture is usually developed before the Applications Architecture.
C. Gap analysis can be used to find omissions in data services and/or data elements.
D. Entity-relationship diagrams should not be used in the Baseline Data Architecture description.
E. Logical data models are rarely used in the Baseline Data Architecture description.

7.9 Recommended Reading

The following are recommended sources of further information for this chapter:

- TOGAF 8.1.1 Enterprise Edition Part II: ADM, Phase C: Information Systems Architectures
- TOGAF 8.1.1 Enterprise Edition Part II: ADM, ADM Input and Output Descriptions

Chapter 8

Data Architecture

8.1 Key Learning Points

This chapter describes the Data Architecture part of Phase C: Information Systems Architectures of the TOGAF Architecture Development Method (ADM).

Key Points Explained

This chapter will help you to answer the following questions:

- What are the objectives of the Data Architecture part of Phase C?
- What does this consist of?
- What is its relationship to the rest of the TOGAF ADM?
- What are the inputs needed for this phase?
- What are the outputs from this phase?

8.2 Objectives

The objective of the Data Architecture within Phase C is to define the types and sources of data needed to support the business, in a way that can be understood by stakeholders. The output should be complete, consistent, and stable.

The work in Phase C: Data Architecture is not concerned with database design. The goal is to define the data entities relevant to the enterprise, not to design logical or physical storage systems.

8.3 Inputs

The inputs to this phase are:

- Data principles, if existing
- Request for Architecture Work
- Statement of Architecture Work

- Architecture Vision
- Relevant technical requirements
- Gap analysis results (from Business Architecture)
- Baseline Business Architecture, Version 1.0 (detailed)
- Target Business Architecture Version 1.0 (detailed)
- Baseline Data Architecture, Version 0.1
- Target Data Architecture, Version 0.1
- Re-usable building blocks, from organization's Enterprise Continuum

8.4 Steps

There are nine steps in this phase.

8.4.1 Develop a Baseline Data Architecture Description
(Syllabus reference 1.CD.1)

The scope and level of detail to be defined depends on the extent to which existing data elements are re-used in the Target Data architecture. Identify the relevant Data Architecture Building Blocks, drawing on the Architecture Continuum, and review the following primitives from the Zachman Framework[1]:

- Business data model (entities, attributes, and relationships)
- Entity-relationship diagrams illustrating views of the Data Architecture
- Logical data model
- Data management process models, including:
  — Data dissemination view
  — Data lifecycle view
  — Data security view
  — Data model management view
- Data entity/business function matrix in the Business Architecture

8.4.2 Review and Select Principles, Reference Models, Viewpoints, and Tools
(Syllabus reference 1.CD.2)

1. Review and/or generate the set of data principles; these will normally form part of an overarching set of architecture principles (see Section 15.2.2)

---

[1] Go to www.zifa.com/framework.html.

2. Select relevant Data Architecture resources (reference models, patterns, etc.) from the Architecture Continuum

3. Select relevant Data Architecture viewpoints such as stakeholders' viewpoints, time dimensions, locations, and business processes; this will enable the architect to demonstrate how stakeholders' concerns are being addressed

4. Identify appropriate tools and techniques to be used for data capture, modeling, and analysis in association with the selected viewpoints; these may be simple documents or sophisticated tools and techniques such as data management models, data models (e.g., IDEF, Object Role Modeling), etc.

8.4.3 Create Data Architecture Model(s)

(Syllabus reference 1.CD.3)

1. For each viewpoint (e.g., the user's viewpoint), create the model for the view (e.g., the software engineering view) required using the selected tool or method; examples of logical data models include the C4ISR Architecture Framework Logical Data Model, the ARTS Data Model for the Retail Industry, and the POSC Data Model for the Petrotechnical industry

2. Check that all stakeholder concerns are covered; if not, create new models or augment existing ones, provide a conceptual data model (by drawing entity-relationship diagrams of entities, attributes, and relationships), a logical data model (logical views of the actual data of interest), and data management process models, including the data dissemination view, data lifecycle view, data security view, and data model management view, and then relate the data entities to the business functions in the Business Architecture

3. Ensure that all information requirements in the Business Architecture are met

4. Perform a trade-off analysis to resolve conflicts among the different views using, for example, CMU/SEI's Architecture Trade-off Analysis Method (ATAM)

5. Check that the models support the principles, objectives, and constraints

6. Note changes to the viewpoint represented in the selected models from the Architecture Continuum, and document

7. Check the architecture models for completeness against requirements

8.4.4   Select Data Architecture Building Blocks
(Syllabus reference 1.CD.4)
1. Identify required building blocks and check against existing library of building blocks, re-using as appropriate
2. Where necessary, define new Data Architecture Building Blocks

8.4.5   Conduct a Checkpoint Review of the Architecture Model
(Syllabus reference 1.CD.5)

Conduct a formal review of the architecture model and building blocks with the stakeholders. Review the entity-business function matrices generated in Step 3 and the Business Architecture generated in Phase B.

8.4.6   Review the Qualitative Criteria
(Syllabus reference 1.CD.6)

Review the qualitative criteria (e.g., integrity, performance, reliability, security, etc.), providing measurable criteria where possible (e.g., mean time to failure and/or minimum tolerable data losses for reliability, etc.). Use the criteria to specify required service levels for data services (for example, via formal Service Level Agreements). The goal is to direct the Applications and Technology Architecture work and the underlying technology for the data.

8.4.7   Complete the Data Architecture
(Syllabus reference 1.CD.7)
1. Select standards for each of the Architecture Building Blocks (ABBs), re-using as much as possible
2. Fully document each ABB
3. Cross-check the overall architecture against the business requirements
4. Document the final requirements traceability report
5. Document the final mapping of the architecture within the Architecture Continuum, identify the ABBs that might be re-used, and publish them via the architecture repository
6. Document the rationale for all building block decisions in the architecture document
7. Prepare the Data Architecture Report (see Section 15.2.14), generate the Data Architecture document (see Section 15.2.13), including the business data model, logical data model, data management process model, data

entity/business function matrix, and data interoperability requirements (e.g., XML schema) – the Data Architecture document should include reports and/or graphics generated by modeling tools to demonstrate key stakeholder views of the architecture – and send the Data Architecture document for review by stakeholders and incorporate feedback

8.4.8 Conduct Checkpoint/Impact Analysis

Check the original motivation for the architecture project and the Statement of Architecture Work against the proposed Data Architecture. Conduct an Impact Analysis to:

1. Identify any areas where the Business Architecture (e.g., business practices) may need to change to cater for changes in the Data Architecture (e.g., changes to forms or databases); if the impact is significant revisit the Business Architecture
2. Identify any areas where the Applications Architecture may need to change to cater for changes in the Data Architecture (or to identify constraints on the Applications Architecture about to be designed); if the impact is significant revisit the Applications Architecture if necessary
3. Identify any constraints on the Technology Architecture
4. Refine the proposed Data Architecture if necessary

8.4.9 Perform Gap Analysis and Create Report
(Syllabus reference 1.CD.8)

At this point a gap analysis should be undertaken and a report generated. A critical source of gaps that should be considered is stakeholder concerns that have been overlooked. Look for data that is not:

- Located where it is needed
- Needed
- Available when needed
- Created
- Consumed

Gap analysis will highlight shortfalls in data services and/or data elements that have been omitted or are yet to be defined; these are known as "gaps". They should either then be explained in a report as correctly eliminated or marked to be addressed by reinstating, developing or procuring the functionality. See Section 15.2.12 for full details of the gap analysis technique including an example.

8.5 Outputs

The outputs of this phase include the following:

- Statement of Architecture Work, updated if necessary
- Baseline Data Architecture, Version 1.0
- Validated data principles, or new data principles (if generated here)
- Target Data Architecture, Version 1.0, including:
  — Business data model
  — Logical data model
  — Data management process models
  — Data entity/business function matrix
  — Data interoperability requirements
- Viewpoints addressing key stakeholder concerns
- Views corresponding to the selected viewpoints; for example:
  — Data dissemination view
  — Data lifecycle view
  — Data security view
  — Data model management view
- Gap analysis results
- Relevant technical requirements that will apply to this evolution of the architecture development cycle
- Data Architecture Report, summarizing what was done and the key findings
- Impact Analysis results
- Updated business requirements

8.6 Summary

The Data Architecture part of Phase C defines the types and sources of data needed to support the business, in a way that can be understood by stakeholders. The architecture team should consider existing relevant data models, such as the ARTS and POSC models.

8.7 Test Yourself Questions

Q1:   Which of the following is not an objective of the Data Architecture part of Phase C?
      A.   To define the types of data needed
      B.   To define the sources of data needed

C. To design a database

D. To produce output that is complete

E. To produce output that is understandable by the stakeholders

Q2: Which of the following is not an input to the Data Architecture part of Phase C?

A. Existing data principles

B. Request for Architecture Change

C. Request for Architecture Work

D. Architecture Vision

E. Gap analysis results from Business Architecture

Q3: Which of the following is not a logical data model that can be used for creating Data Architecture models for views?

A. C4ISR Architecture Framework Logical Data Model

B. ARTS

C. POSC

D. Zachman

E. All of these

Q4: Which of the following is the next step in the Data Architecture part of Phase C after the Data Architecture Building Blocks have been selected?

A. Complete the Data Architecture

B. Checkpoint/Impact Analysis

C. Gap analysis

D. Create Data Architecture models

E. Conduct a checkpoint review

Q5: Which of the following statements is false? Gap analysis in the Data Architecture part of Phase C:

A. Identifies data that is not processed according to the performance metrics

B. Identifies new Architecture Building Blocks for procurement or building

C. Identifies accidental omissions in the new architecture

D. Identifies data that is not located where it is needed

E. Identifies data that is not consumed

8.8 Recommended Reading

The following are recommended sources of further information for this chapter:

- TOGAF 8.1.1 Enterprise Edition Part II: ADM, Phase C: Information Systems Architectures – Data Architecture
- TOGAF 8.1.1 Enterprise Edition Part II: ADM, ADM Input and Output Descriptions
- TOGAF 8.1.1 Enterprise Edition Part IV: Resource Base, Developing Architecture Views

Chapter 9

Phase C: Applications Architecture

9.1 Key Learning Points

This chapter describes the Applications Architecture part of Phase C: Information Systems Architectures of the TOGAF Architecture Development Method (ADM).

Key Points Explained

This chapter will help you to answer the following questions:
- What are the objectives of the Applications Architecture part of Phase C?
- What does this consist of?
- What is its relationship to the rest of the TOGAF ADM?
- What are the inputs needed for this phase?
- What are the outputs from this phase?

9.2 Objectives

The objective of this phase is to define the *kinds* of application systems necessary to process the data and support the business.

Note that this is *not* concerned with applications systems design. The goal is to define what kinds of application systems are relevant and what those applications need to do. The applications are not described as computer systems but as logical groups of capabilities that manage data and support business functions. The applications and their capabilities should be defined without reference to particular technologies. The applications should be stable (whereas the technology used to implement them may not be).

9.3 Inputs

The inputs to this phase are:
- Application principles, if existing
- Request for Architecture Work

- Statement of Architecture Work
- Architecture Vision
- Relevant technical requirements
- Gap analysis results (from Phase B: Business Architecture)
- Baseline Business Architecture, Version 1.0 (detailed)
- Target Business Architecture, Version 1.0 (detailed)
- Re-usable building blocks, from organization's Enterprise Continuum (see Chapter 18)
- Baseline Applications Architecture, Version 0.1
- Target Applications Architecture, Version 0.1

9.4 Steps

There are eight steps in this phase.

9.4.1 Develop a Baseline Applications Architecture Description
(Syllabus reference 1.CA.1)

Develop a Baseline Description of the existing Applications Architecture, to the extent necessary to support the Target Applications Architecture. The scope and level of detail to be defined will depend on the extent to which existing application components are likely to be re-used and on existing architecture descriptions. Define for each application:

- Name (short and long)
- Maintainer
- Owner(s)/business unit(s) responsible for requirements
- Other users
- Plain language description of what the application does (not how it does it)
- Status (planned, operational, obsolete)
- Business functions supported
- Organizational units supported
- Hardware/software platform(s)
- Networks used
- Precedent and successor applications

Identify the relevant Applications Architecture Building Blocks, drawing on the Architecture Continuum. Sometimes a group of applications can be considered as a building block; sometimes a single application might be a building block.

9.4.2 Review and Validate Application Principles – Select Reference Models, Viewpoints, and Tools
(Syllabus reference 1.CA.2)

The application principles developed as part of the set of architecture principles in earlier phases should be reviewed and validated. Select relevant Applications Architecture resources (reference models, patterns, etc.) from the Architecture Continuum. Also select relevant Applications Architecture viewpoints; i.e., those that will enable the architect to demonstrate how stakeholder concerns are being addressed. Then identify appropriate tools and techniques to be used for capture, modeling, and analysis, in association with the selected viewpoints. Consider using platform-independent descriptions of business logic. For example, the OMG's Model-Driven Architecture (MDA) offers an approach to modeling Applications Architectures that protects business logic from changes to technology.

Typical viewpoints that should be considered include: those relevant to functional and individual users of applications, the software engineering view, the application-to-application communication view, the software distribution view, and the enterprise management view.

9.4.3 Create Architecture Models for each Viewpoint
(Syllabus reference 1.CA.3)

1. For each viewpoint, create the model for the specific view required
2. Ensure that all stakeholder concerns are covered; if not, create new models or augment existing models – model at least the Common Applications services view and the Applications Interoperability view of assumptions, dependencies, and standards (The Open Group has a Reference Model for Integrated Information Infrastructure that can be used here)
3. Relate the application systems to the business functions in the Business Architecture; this can be complicated, and involves generating application-business function matrices tabulating all the relationships and using the business function-to-organizational unit mappings contained in the Business Architecture

4. Ensure that all information requirements in the Business Architecture are met
5. Perform trade-off analysis to resolve conflicts among the different views, using, for example, CMU/SEI's Architecture Trade-off Analysis Method (ATAM)
6. Check that the models support the principles, objectives, and constraints
7. Note changes to the viewpoint represented in the selected models from the Architecture Continuum, and document
8. Test architecture models for completeness against requirements

9.4.4 Identify Candidate Applications
(Syllabus reference 1.CA.4)

1. Review the re-usable Architecture Building Blocks and Solution Building Blocks from the enterprise's Architecture Continuum, the business scenario description, and the Baseline Description; list all potential application systems
2. Review the entity-to-business function matrices from the Data Architecture and identify potential applications to perform the required data management functions and/or to automate particular business functions
3. Even if a complete Data Architecture is not available, review all existing lists of data
4. Develop a user location/applications matrix
5. Consider other potential application systems based on innovative use of new technology
6. Merge all lists into a single list of candidate application systems, including for each a brief description of business function(s) supported and data information managed
7. Create application definitions for all candidate application systems; for each application:
   a. Assign a unique name and identifier
   b. Write a brief description of what the application does (not how it works)
   c. Write a brief description of its business benefits
   d. Simplify complicated applications by decomposing them into two or more applications

e. Ensure that the set of application definitions is internally consistent, by removing duplicate functionality as far as possible, and combining similar applications into one

f. Identify technology requirements and candidate technology building blocks, where this affects the applications design, including re-usable s Building Blocks from the enterprise's Architecture Continuum and external components

g. Identify any critical infrastructure dependencies (e.g., operating system and network services)

h. Identify and minimize any critical application dependencies

i. Relate the applications to the files and databases described in the Baseline Description and/or to the data entities defined in the Data Architecture

j. Draw diagrams to illustrate views of the Applications Architecture relevant to different stakeholders

9.4.5 Conduct a Checkpoint Review
(Syllabus reference 1.CA.5)

At this stage, a formal checkpoint review should be held of the application-business function matrices generated in Step 3, and the Business Architecture generated in Phase B with the stakeholders.

9.4.6 Review the Qualitative Criteria
(Syllabus reference 1.CA.6)

Review the qualitative criteria, providing as many measurable criteria as possible (e.g., privacy/confidentiality, reliability, minimum tolerable outages, cycle requirements and transaction volume requirements at peak and mean times, numbers and locations of users, etc.). Use these criteria to specify required service levels for applications services (for example, via formal Service Level Agreements).

9.4.7 Complete the Applications Architecture
(Syllabus reference 1.CA.7)

1. Select standards for each of the Architecture Building Blocks (ABBs), re-using as much as possible from the reference models selected from the Architecture Continuum

2. Fully document each ABB
3. Do a final cross-check of the overall architecture against the business requirements; document rationale for building block decisions in the architecture document
4. Document final requirements traceability report
5. Document final mapping of the architecture within the Architecture Continuum; from the selected ABBs identify those that might be re-used and publish via the architecture repository
6. Document rationale for building block decisions in the architecture document
7. Prepare the Applications Architecture Report (see Section 15.2.16); generate the Applications Architecture document (see Section 15.2.15); use reports and/or graphics to demonstrate key views of the architecture; send the Applications Architecture document for review by stakeholders and incorporate feedback
8. Checkpoint/Impact Analysis: Check the original motivation for the architecture project and the Statement of Architecture Work against the proposed Applications Architecture; conduct an Impact Analysis; identify any areas where the Business Architecture (e.g., business practices) may need to change to cater for changes in the Applications Architecture (for example, changes to forms or procedures, application systems, or database systems); if the impact is significant this may require the Business Architecture to be revisited; identify any areas where the Data Architecture (if generated at this point) may need to change to cater for changes in the Applications Architecture (or to identify constraints on the Data Architecture, if about to be designed); identify any constraints on the Technology Architecture about to be designed

9.4.8 Perform Gap Analysis and Create Report
(Syllabus reference 1.CA.8)

At this point, a gap analysis should be undertaken and a report generated. Gap analysis in this phase will highlight shortfalls in applications services and/or applications components that have been accidentally left out, deliberately eliminated, or are yet to be defined. See Section 15.2.12 for full details of the gap analysis technique including an example.

9.5 Outputs

The outputs of this phase include the following:

- Statement of Architecture Work (updated if necessary)
- Baseline Applications Architecture, Version 1.0
- Validated application principles, or new application principles (if generated here)
- Target Applications Architecture, Version 1.0, including:
  — Process Systems Model
  — Place Systems Model
  — Time Systems Model
  — People Systems Model
  — Applications interoperability requirements
- Viewpoints addressing key stakeholder concerns
- Views corresponding to the selected viewpoints; for example:
  — Common Applications Services view
  — Applications Interoperability view
  — Applications/Information view
  — Applications/User Locations view
- Gap analysis results
- Applications Architecture Report, summarizing what was done and the key findings
- Impact Analysis:
  — Areas where the Business Architecture may need to change
  — Areas where the Data Architecture may need to change
  — Constraints on the Technology Architecture
- Updated business requirements

9.6 Summary

The objective of this phase is to define the *kinds* of application systems necessary to process the data and support the business. The goal is to define what kinds of application systems are relevant and what those applications need to do. The applications are not described as computer systems but as logical groups of capabilities that manage data and support business functions. Thus, the applications and their capabilities should be defined without reference to particular technologies. The applications should be stable, whereas the technology used to implement them may not be.

9.7 Test Yourself Questions

Q1:   How should the application systems best be described?
- A.   As computer systems
- B.   As logical groups of capabilities
- C.   As schemas
- D.   As data-flow diagrams
- E.   As UML diagrams

Q2:   When resolving conflicts amongst views, which technique can be used?
- A.   Gap Analysis
- B.   Trade-off Analysis
- C.   Impact Analysis
- D.   Prince 2
- E.   Resource-Event-Agent business models

Q3:   Which of the following is not a suggested viewpoint for the Applications Architecture part of Phase C?
- A.   Software engineering
- B.   Functional users of applications
- C.   Enterprise management
- D.   Financial
- E.   Application-to-application communication

Q4:   Which of the following is not suggested by TOGAF for inclusion in the Baseline Applications Architecture Description for each application?
- A.   Name of the application
- B.   Licensing status of the application
- C.   Platform dependencies
- D.   Name of the maintainer
- E.   Description of the application in plain language

Q5:   What is the next step in the Applications Architecture part of Phase C after reference models and viewpoints have been selected?
- A.   Develop an Applications Architecture Baseline Description
- B.   Identify candidate applications
- C.   Create architecture models for each viewpoint

    D.   Conduct a checkpoint review

    E.   Review non-functional criteria

9.8 Recommended Reading

The following are recommended sources of further information for this chapter:

- TOGAF 8.1.1 Enterprise Edition Part II: ADM, Phase C: Information Systems Architectures – Applications Architecture
- TOGAF 8.1.1 Enterprise Edition Part II: ADM, ADM Input and Output Descriptions
- TOGAF 8.1.1 Enterprise Edition Part IV: Resource Base, Developing Architecture Views

Chapter 10

Phase D: Technology Architecture

10.1 Key Learning Points

This chapter describes Phase D: Technology Architecture of the TOGAF
Architecture Development Method (ADM).

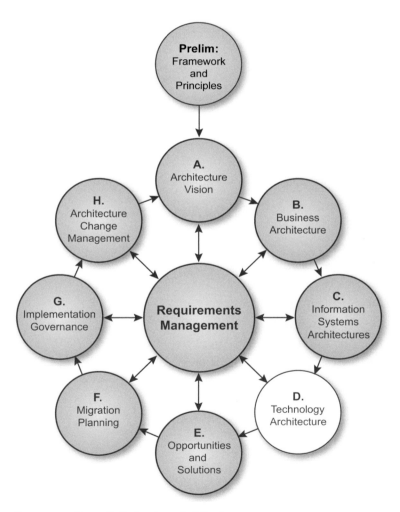

Figure 10.1: Phase D: Technology Architecture

Key Points Explained

This chapter will help you to answer the following questions:

- What are the objectives of the Phase D?
- What does Phase D consist of?
- What is its relationship to the rest of the TOGAF ADM?
- What are the inputs needed for Phase D?
- What are the outputs from Phase D?

10.2 Objectives

The objective of this phase is to develop a Technology Architecture that will form the basis of the following implementation work.

10.3 Inputs

The inputs to this phase are:

- Technology principles, if existing
- Request for Architecture Work
- Statement of Architecture Work
- Architecture Vision
- Baseline Technology Architecture, Version 0.1
- Target Technology Architecture, Version 0.1
- Relevant technical requirements from previous phases
- Gap analysis results (from Data Architecture)
- Gap analysis results (from Applications Architecture)
- Baseline Business Architecture, Version 1.0 (detailed)
- Baseline Data Architecture, Version 1.0
- Baseline Applications Architecture, Version 1.0
- Target Business Architecture, Version 1.0 (detailed)
- Re-usable building blocks, from organization's Enterprise Continuum
- Target Data Architecture, Version 1.0
- Target Applications Architecture, Version 1.0

10.4 Steps Overview

This phase has nine steps, the first of which is to create the Baseline Technology Architecture and the remaining eight to create the Target Technology Architecture.

10.4.1 Create Baseline Technology Architecture Description
(Syllabus reference 1.D.1)

The first step in this phase focuses on defining the Baseline Technology Architecture as follows:

1. Review Baseline Business Architecture, Baseline Data Architecture, and Baseline Applications Architecture for information
2. Develop a Baseline Description of the existing Technology Architecture; the scope and level of detail needed depends on whether existing components will be re-used in the Target Technology Architecture; define for each major hardware or software platform:
   a. Name (short and long)
   b. Physical location
   c. Owner(s)
   d. Other users
   e. Plain language description of what the hardware/software platform is and what it is used for
   f. Business functions supported
   g. Organizational units supported
   h. Networks accessed
   i. Applications and data supported
   j. System inter-dependencies
3. Identify and document candidate Technology Architecture Building Blocks
4. Draft the Technology Architecture Baseline report: summarize key findings and conclusions, developing suitable graphics and schematics to illustrate baseline configuration(s); if warranted, provide individual Technology Architecture Baseline Descriptions as annexes
5. Send the Baseline Technology Architecture Report to relevant stakeholders for review and incorporate feedback; refine the Baseline Description only if necessary

10.4.2 Create Target Technology Architecture
(Syllabus reference 1.D.2)

There are eight steps to create the Target Technology Architecture. They are described in their own subsections of this chapter since there are a large number of activities in each step.

10.5 Target Technology Architecture Detailed Steps

10.5.1 Step 1: Create a Baseline Technology Architecture Description
(Syllabus reference 1.D.2.1)

10.5.1.1 Objective
The objective is to convert the description of the existing system into
"services terminology" using the TOGAF Foundation Architecture's TRM
(see Chapter 16). The rationale is to structure the existing system description
to make it compatible with standards and descriptions used within the
Foundation Architecture.

10.5.1.2 Approach
Architecture Building Blocks (ABBs) should be used to show how the
architecture could be implemented. Their functionality is defined without
referring to specific products (see Section 15.2.21). ABBs should be
documented and stored to maximize re-use. A list of questions should be
produced to help measure the effectiveness of the new architecture.

10.5.1.3 Inputs
The inputs to this step are:
- Technology principles
- Request for Architecture Work
- Statement of Architecture Work
- Architecture Vision
- Baseline Technology Architecture, Version 0.1
- Target Technology Architecture, Version 0.1
- Relevant technical requirements from previous phases
- Gap analysis results (from Data Architecture)
- Gap analysis results (from Applications Architecture)
- Baseline Business Architecture, Version 1.0
- Baseline Data Architecture, Version 1.0
- Baseline Applications Architecture, Version 1.0
- Business Architecture, Version 1.0
- Re-usable building blocks, from the organization's Enterprise Continuum
- Target Data Architecture, Version 1.0
- Target Applications Architecture, Version 1.0
- Re-usable Architecture Building Blocks, from your organization's

Architecture Continuum
- Re-usable Solution Building Blocks, from your organization's Solutions
  Continuum

10.5.1.4 Activities
The key activities in this step are:
- Collect data on current system
- Document all constraints
- Review/produce and validate the Technology Architecture principles;
  these will normally form part of the architecture principles (see Part IV:
  Resource Base, Architecture Principles)
- List distinct functionality
- Produce affinity groupings of functionality using TOGAF TRM service
  groupings (or your business' Foundation Architecture)
- Analyze relationships between groupings
- Sanity-check functionality to ensure all of the current system is considered
- Identify the interfaces
- Produce the Technology Architecture model
- Verify the Technology Architecture model
- Document key questions to test the merits of the Technology Architecture
- Document criteria for selection of service portfolio architecture

10.5.1.5 Outputs
The outputs of this step are:
- Technology principles
- Baseline Technology Architecture, Version 1.0
- Target Technology Architecture, Version 0.2, including:
  — Technology Architecture – constraints
  — Technology Architecture – architecture principles
  — Technology Architecture – requirements traceability, key questions list
  — Technology Architecture – requirements traceability, criteria for
    selection of service portfolio
  — Technology Architecture Model, Version 0.1

10.5.2 Step 2: Consider Different Architecture Reference Models, Viewpoints, and Tools
(Syllabus reference 1.D.2.2)

10.5.2.1 Objective

The objective is to perform an analysis of the Technology Architecture from a number of different viewpoints and to document the result. The purpose is to ensure that all relevant stakeholder concerns have been considered in the final Technology Architecture.

10.5.2.2 Approach

The Business Architecture is used to select the relevant viewpoints. These are created first from the existing system to identify the current systems requirements that the stakeholders say must be satisfied. A set of stakeholder viewpoints must also be created for the target system. The corresponding views of the existing system will be compared with the views of the target system to identify elements of the existing system that are intended for replacement or improvement. Several different viewpoints may be useful (see TOGAF 8.1.1 Enterprise Edition Part IV: Resource Base, Developing Architecture Views).

10.5.2.3 Inputs

The inputs to this step are:
- Request for Architecture Work
- Statement of Architecture Work
- Target Business Architecture, Version 1.0
- Target Technology Architecture, Version 0.2

10.5.2.4 Activities

The key activities in this step are:
1. Select relevant Technology Architecture resources (reference models, patterns, etc.) from the Architecture Continuum using business drivers, stakeholders, and concerns
2. Select relevant Technology Architecture viewpoints; i.e., those that enable the architect to demonstrate how stakeholder concerns are addressed (see Section 15.2.19):
   a. Document the selected viewpoints using a guide such as ANSI/IEEE Std 1471-2000
   b. Reference models include the TOGAF TRM
   c. Consider developing at least the following views: Networked Computing/Hardware, Communications, Processing, Cost, Standards
   d. Brainstorm and document technical constraints and ensure they are covered by the viewpoints

3. Identify appropriate tools and techniques to be used for capture, modeling, and analysis together with the selected viewpoints
4. Perform trade-off analysis to resolve conflicts using, for example, CMU/ SEI's Architecture Trade-off Analysis Method (ATAM)

Brainstorm

A brainstorm is a creativity technique of generating ideas to solve a problem and can be done either individually or in a group. In group brainstorming, the participants are encouraged, and often expected, to share their ideas with one another as soon as they are generated. The key to brainstorming is to not interrupt the thought process. As ideas come to mind, they are captured and stimulate the development of better ideas.

(Source: wikipedia.org)

10.5.2.5 Outputs

The outputs of this step are:

- Target Technology Architecture, Version 0.3, comprising:
  — Technology Architecture – architecture viewpoints
  — Networked Computing/Hardware view
  — Communications view
  — Processing view
  — Cost view
  — Standards view
  — Technology Architecture – constraints

10.5.3 Step 3: Create an Architecture Model of Building Blocks
(Syllabus reference 1.D.2.3)

10.5.3.1 Objective

The objective is to create an architecture model and to determine how the services required will be grouped after considering the viewpoints.

10.5.3.2 Approach

The broad architecture model starts as a TOGAF TRM-based model derived from the service-to-function mapping done in Step 1. Modifications can be made to the TOGAF TRM to create an organization-specific TRM.

This step models the building blocks needed. Once the architecture model is created it must be checked for coverage and completeness. For each building block determine its impact and note the rationale for decisions, including decisions not to do things.

10.5.3.3 Inputs

The inputs to this step are:
- Target Business Architecture, Version 1.0
- Target Technology Architecture, Version 0.3
  — Technology Architecture – viewpoints
  — Technology Architecture – constraints
- Re-usable Architecture Building Blocks, from your organization's Architecture Continuum

10.5.3.4 Activities

The key activities in this step are:
1. Identify the relevant Technology Architecture Building Blocks, drawing on the Architecture Continuum
2. For each viewpoint, create the model for the specific view required, using the selected tool or method; consider developing at least the following five views: Networked Computing/Hardware, Communications, Processing, Cost, Standards
3. Check that all stakeholder concerns are covered, creating or augmenting models if necessary
4. Ensure that all information requirements in the Business Architecture, Data Architecture, and Applications Architecture are met
5. Perform trade-off analysis to resolve conflicts among the different views, using, for example, CMU/SEI's Architecture Trade-off Analysis Method (ATAM)
6. Check that the models support the principles, objectives, and constraints
7. Note changes to the viewpoint represented in the selected models from the Architecture Continuum, and document
8. Identify Solution Building Blocks that could be used to implement the system and model them
9. Check building blocks against existing library of building blocks and re-use as appropriate
10. Test architecture models for completeness against requirements
11. Document rationale for building block decisions in the architecture document

10.5.3.5 Outputs

The outputs of this step are:

- Target Technology Architecture, Version 0.4
  - Technology Architecture Model, with Networked Computing/ Hardware, Communications, Processing, Cost, and Standards views
  - Technology Architecture – change requests and/or extensions or amendments to be incorporated in an organization-specific Architecture Continuum

10.5.4 Step 4: Select the Services Portfolio Required per Building Block
(Syllabus reference 1.D.2.4)

10.5.4.1 Objective

The objective is to select service portfolios for each building block generated in Step 3. Service portfolios are combinations of basic service categories in the TRM that do not conflict.

10.5.4.2 Approach

For each ABB, build up a service description portfolio. The set of services must be checked to ensure that the functionality provided meets the requirements.

10.5.4.3 Inputs

The inputs to this step are:

- Target Business Architecture, Version 1.0
- Target Technology Architecture, Version 0.4
- Technical Reference Model (TRM)
- Standards Information Base (SIB)

10.5.4.4 Activities

The key activities in this step are:

1. Produce affinity grouping of services
2. Cross-check affinity groups against needs
3. Document service description portfolio for each ABB, cross-checking for non-conflicting services
4. Document change requests to architectures in the Architecture Continuum

10.5.4.5 Outputs

The outputs of this step are:

- Target Technology Architecture, Version 0.5
  - Technology Architecture – target services
  - Technology Architecture – change requests and/or extensions or amendments to be incorporated in an organization-specific Architecture Continuum

10.5.5 Step 5: Confirm that the Business Goals and Objectives are Met
(Syllabus reference 1.D.2.5)

10.5.5.1 Objective

The objective is to clarify and check the business goals and other objectives. This is required as a cross-check that the Technology Architecture meets these objectives.

10.5.5.2 Approach

The key question list is used to test the merit and completeness of the architecture model and service description portfolio.

10.5.5.3 Inputs

The inputs to this step are:

- Target Business Architecture, Version 1.0 (business goals)
- Target Technology Architecture, Version 0.5

10.5.5.4 Activities

The key activities in this step are:

1. Conduct a formal checkpoint review of the architecture model and building blocks with stakeholders, checking that business goals are met; ensure that the architecture addresses each question in the key questions list
2. Document findings

10.5.5.5 Outputs

The outputs of this step are:

- Technology Architecture, Version 0.6
  - Technology Architecture – requirements traceability (business objectives criteria)

10.5.6 Step 6: Choose the Criteria for Specification Selection
(Syllabus reference 1.D.2.6)

10.5.6.1 Objective
The objective of this step is to choose a set of criteria for selecting specifications and portfolios of specifications.

10.5.6.2 Approach
The criteria chosen will depend on the existing system and the overall objectives for the new architecture. The objectives should be developed from the organization's business goals (see TOGAF 8.1.1 Enterprise Edition Part IV: Resource Base, Business Scenarios). A high level of consensus is often considered the most important factor because standards and specifications have to accommodate a wide range of user needs; see Example 10-1 and Example 10-2.

Example 10.1: Criteria for Specification Selection

The US National Institute for Standards and Technology (NIST) uses international standards for the basis of specifications. The process through which these international standards have evolved req uires a very high level of consensus. A number of US Federal Information Processing Standards (FIPS) specified in the Application Portability Profile (APP) are based on approved international standards.

Example 10.2: Criteria for Specification Selection

A standard or specification:
- Must meet the organization's requirements
- Must meet legal requirements
- Should be a publicly available specification
- Should have been developed by a process which sought a high level of consensus from a wide variety of sources
- Should be supported by a range of readily available products
- Should be complete
- Should be a well understood, mature technology
- Should be testable, so that components or products can be checked for conformance
- Should support internationalization
- Should have no serious implications for ongoing support of legacy systems
- Should be stable
- Should be in wide use
- Should have few, if any, problems or limitations

(These criteria were selected by a large government organization with the intention of building a stable and widely applicable architecture.)

10.5.6.3 Inputs

The inputs to this step are:

- Target Business Architecture, Version 1.0
- Target Technology Architecture, Version 0.6
- Standards Information Base (SIB)

10.5.6.4 Activities

The key activities in this step are:

1. Brainstorm criteria for choosing specifications and portfolios of specifications relying on previously used criteria for existing system and extrapolating for new architecture elements
2. Meet with sponsors and present current work to negotiate continuation

10.5.6.5 Outputs

The outputs of this step are:

- Target Technology Architecture, Version 0.7, showing requirements traceability (standards selection criteria)

10.5.7 Step 7: Complete the Architecture Definition
(Syllabus reference 1.D.2.7)

10.5.7.1 Objective

The objective is to fully specify the Technology Architecture. This is a complex and iterative process.

10.5.7.2 Approach

The architecture definition may be completed in two steps: define an intermediate Transitional Architecture then the final Target Architecture. The specification of building blocks as a portfolio of services is described below.

- The earliest building block definitions start relatively abstract, defined by standards and services that map to the architecture framework
- Once a model and a portfolio of services have been established, select the set of specifications that provide the services and that can be combined to create the building blocks
- Check that the organization-specific requirements will be met; check dependencies and boundaries of functions and determine what products are available; for an example see TOGAF 8.1.1 Enterprise Edition Part IV: Resource Base, Building Blocks

Building blocks can be defined at a number of levels:

- — Fundamental functionality and attributes
- — Interfaces – chosen set, supplied (APIs, data formats, protocols, hardware interfaces, standards)
- — Dependent building blocks with required functionality
- — Map to business/organizational entities and policies
- Finally, the building blocks become more implementation-specific as Solution Building Blocks (SBBs) and their interfaces become the detailed architecture specification. SBBs are a way to determine how portions of the Target Architecture might be procured, developed, or re-used.

A full list of standards and specifications recommended by The Open Group can be found in the Standards Information Base (see Chapter 17).

10.5.7.3 Inputs
The inputs to this step are:
- Target Business Architecture, Version 1.0
- Target Technology Architecture, Version 0.7
- Re-usable Architecture Building Blocks, from your organization's Architecture Continuum
- Standards Information Base (SIB)

10.5.7.4 Activities
The key activities in this step are:
1. Ensure clear documentation of all interfaces for each building block (APIs, data formats, protocols, hardware interfaces)
2. Select standards for each of the Architecture Building Blocks, re-using as much as possible from the reference models
3. Fully document each Architecture Building Block
4. Cross-check the overall architecture against business requirements; document rationale for building block decisions in the architecture document
5. Document final requirements traceability report
6. Document final mapping of the architecture within the Architecture Continuum; from the selected Architecture Building Blocks, identify those that might be re-used and publish via the architecture repository
7. Document rationale for building block decisions in the architecture document
8. Generate the Technology Architecture document

9. Prepare the Technology Architecture Report; send the Technology
    Architecture document to stakeholders and incorporate feedback
10. Checkpoint/Impact Analysis: Check the original motivation and
    Statement of Architecture Work against the proposed Technology
    Architecture; conduct an Impact Analysis to cater for changes in
    the Technology Architecture; check whether the Business, Data, or
    Applications Architectures need to change

10.5.7.5 Outputs
The outputs of this step are:
- Target Technology Architecture, Version 0.8
  — Technology Architecture – architecture specification
  — Technology Architecture – requirements traceability
  — Technology Architecture – mapping of the architectures in the
    Architecture Continuum
  — Technology Architecture Report

10.5.8 Step 8: Conduct a Gap Analysis
(Syllabus reference 1.D.2.8)

10.5.8.1 Objective
The objective is to identify areas of the current and target system for which
provision has not been made in the Technology Architecture.

10.5.8.2 Approach
At this point a gap analysis should be undertaken and a report generated.
See Section 15.2.12 for full details of the gap analysis technique including an
example.

10.5.8.3 Inputs
The inputs to this step are:
- Target Business Architecture, Version 1.0
- Target Technology Architecture, Version 0.8
- Target Data Architecture, Version 1.0
- Target Applications Architecture, Version 1.0

10.5.8.4 Activities

The key activities in this step are:

1. Create gap matrix
2. Identify building blocks to be carried over, classifying as either changed or unchanged
3. Identify eliminated building blocks
4. Identify new building blocks
5. Identify gaps and classify as those that should be developed, those that should be procured, and those inherited

10.5.8.5 Outputs

The outputs of this step are:

- Target Technology Architecture, Version 1.0
- Technology Architecture – gap analysis report

10.6 Outputs

The outputs of this phase are:

- Statement of Architecture Work, updated if necessary
- Baseline Technology Architecture, Version 1.0
- Validated technology principles or new technology principles (if generated here)
- Technology Architecture Report, summarizing what was done and the key findings
- Target Technology Architecture, Version 1.0
- Technology Architecture, gap analysis report
- Viewpoints addressing key stakeholder concerns
- Views corresponding to the selected viewpoints

10.7 Summary

The objective of Phase D: Technology Architecture is to document the fundamental organization of an IT system, embodied in its hardware, software, and communications technology, their relationships to each other and the environment, and the principles governing its design and evolution. The key steps are as follows:

- Analyze the existing system in consistent terms, using terminology from the TOGAF Technical Reference Model (TRM)

- Document the explicit requirements from earlier phases, together with implicit concerns from different viewpoints
- Define models in terms of functionality, and validate against requirements
- Select services and define interface standards
- Build a list of possible projects

10.8 Test Yourself Questions

Q1: Which of the following statements best describes the objective of Phase D?
   A. To develop a Business Architecture
   B. To develop a Technology Architecture
   C. To develop an Applications Architecture
   D. To develop a Data Architecture
   E. To evaluate the Technology Architecture

Q2: Which of the following is not an input from an earlier phase of the ADM into Phase D?
   A. The Baseline Technology Architecture
   B. The Baseline Business Architecture
   C. Technical Requirements
   D. The TOGAF TRM
   E. Re-usable Building Blocks from the Enterprise Continuum

Q3: Which of the following is not a step in Phase D?
   A. Select services
   B. Create architecture model
   C. Confirm business objectives
   D. Consider views
   E. Implementation Recommendations

Q4: Which of the following is not a part of the Baseline Technology Architecture Description?
   A. A review of the Baseline Information Systems Architecture
   B. A definition of each major hardware and software platform type
   C. A draft report summarizing the Baseline Technology Architecture
   D. A review of the draft Baseline Technology Architecture Report
   E. A review of non-functional criteria

Q5:   Which of the following views is not suggested by TOGAF when creating viewpoints for architecture models in Phase D: Technology Architecture?

A.   Standards

B.   Costs

C.   Logical data model

D.   Communications

E.   Networking

10.9 Recommended Reading

The following are recommended sources of further information for this chapter:

- TOGAF 8.1.1 Enterprise Edition Part II: ADM, Phase D: Technology Architecture
- TOGAF 8.1.1 Enterprise Edition Part II: ADM, ADM Input and Output Descriptions
- TOGAF 8.1.1 Enterprise Edition Part IV: Resource Base, Developing Architecture Views

Chapter 11

Phase E: Opportunities and Solutions

11.1 Key Learning Points

This chapter describes Phase E: Opportunities and Solutions of the TOGAF Architecture Development Method (ADM).

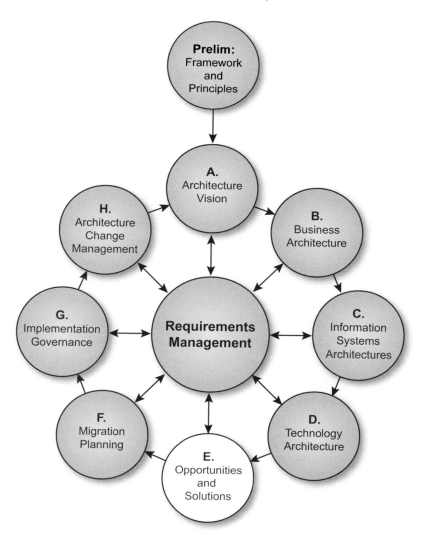

Figure 11.1: Phase E: Opportunities and Solutions

Key Points Explained
This chapter will help you to answer the following questions:
- What are the objectives of Phase E?
- What does Phase E consist of?
- What is its relationship to the rest of the TOGAF ADM?
- What are the inputs needed for Phase E?
- What are the outputs from Phase E?

11.2 Objectives

The objectives of Phase E are as follows:
- Evaluate and select implementation options (for example, build *versus* buy *versus* re-use)
- Identify the strategic parameters for change and the projects to be undertaken
- Assess the costs and benefits of the projects
- Generate an overall implementation and migration strategy and a detailed Implementation Plan

11.3 Approach

Phase E is the first phase which is directly concerned with implementation. It identifies the parameters of change, the phases, and the necessary projects using the gap analysis on the business functions in the old environment (baseline) and the new (target) that was created in Phase D. The output will form the basis of the Implementation Plan. This phase also identifies new business opportunities. If existing functions need modification, then one possibility is to leave an existing system in place, co-existing with the new. The main problems with this are:
- User interfaces: combining user interfaces from the old and new applications in a single unit can be difficult.
- Access to data: often the new and old applications need to share data. This can be difficult unless the old and new systems use the same database technology.
- Connectivity: this may involve expenditure on software and gateway equipment. Sometimes the old system is simply too out-of-date for current connectivity solutions.

It is also necessary to verify that the organization-specific requirements will be met by checking against the business scenario that is driving the scope of the whole project. Note that the ensuing development must include recognition of dependencies and boundaries for functions and should take account of the products that are available.

> The most successful strategy for Phase E is to focus on projects that will deliver short-term pay-offs and so create an impetus for proceeding with longer-term projects.

11.4 Inputs

The inputs to this phase are:

- Request for Architecture Work
- Statement of Architecture Work
- Target Business Architecture, Version 1.0
- Target Data Architecture, Version 1.0
- Target Applications Architecture, Version 1.0
- Target Technology Architecture, Version 1.0
- Re-usable Architecture Building Blocks from your organization's Enterprise Continuum
- Product information

11.5 Steps

11.5.1 Identify the Key Business Drivers
(Syllabus reference: 1.E.1)

The first step is to identify the key business drivers constraining the sequence of implementation. Typical factors that might be taken into consideration include reduction of costs, consolidation of services, introduction of new customer services, etc.

11.5.2   Review Gap Analysis
(Syllabus reference: 1.E.2)

The gap analysis report generated in Phase D: Technology Architecture should then be reviewed to determine what is missing, and what needs to be added to complete the architecture.

11.5.3   Brainstorm Technical Requirements
(Syllabus reference: 1.E.3)

Technical requirements from a functional perspective should be produced. This can be done through a brainstorming session.

11.5.4   Brainstorm Other Requirements
(Syllabus reference: 1.E.4)

Requirements for co-existence and interoperability should be produced. Again, it is recommended that this be done through a brainstorming session.

11.5.5   Architecture Assessment and Gap Analysis
(Syllabus reference: 1.E.5)

Perform architecture assessment and gap analysis.

11.5.6   Identify Work Packages or Projects
(Syllabus reference: 1.E.6)

The final step is to identify work packages or projects and to classify them. Recommended classifications are:

- New development
- Procurement
- Re-use of existing system

This list of projects is then added to the Impact Analysis document, which is an output of this phase.

11.6 Outputs

The outputs of this phase are:

- Implementation and migration strategy
- High-level Implementation Plan
- Impact Analysis document – the project list section is documented in this phase (see Section 15.2.23)

11.7 Summary

Phase E is the first phase which is directly concerned with implementation. It identifies the parameters of change, the phases, and the necessary projects using gap analysis on the business functions in the old environment and the new. The output forms the basis of the Implementation Plan.

11.8 Test Yourself Questions

Q1: Phase E is the first phase concerned with:
- A. Defining the implementation
- B. Defining the architecture framework and key architecture principles
- C. Setting the scope, constraints, and expectations for the project
- D. Validating the business context
- E. Analyzing the cost, benefits, and risk

Q2: What deliverable from Phase D: Technology Architecture is the most important in Phase E?
- A. Updated Requirements
- B. Technology Architecture Report
- C. Impact Analysis
- D. Gap Analysis
- E. Updated Business Architecture

Q3: Which of the following is not an objective of Phase E?
- A. Evaluate and select implementation options
- B. Prioritize the implementation projects
- C. Identify the top-level projects
- D. Assess the costs and benefits of the projects
- E. Generate an overall implementation and migration strategy and a detailed Implementation Plan

Q4:   Which technique should be used to identify the parameters of change
      and the necessary projects in Phase E?
      A.   Impact Analysis
      B.   Migration Planning
      C.   Brainstorming session
      D.   Gap Analysis
      E.   Business Scenarios

Q5:   Which of the following is the most successful strategy for Phase E?
      A.   Focus on the application systems that are relevant to the
           enterprise
      B.   Focus on projects that will deliver short-term payoffs
      C.   Focus on top-down development
      D.   Reverse engineering
      E.   Trial and error

Q6:   Which of the following statements about Phase E is true?
      A.   Coexistence of the old and new systems is straightforward.
      B.   Projects that deliver short-term pay-offs should be given low
           priority.
      C.   One of the inputs to this phase is the Architecture Vision.
      D.   One of the inputs to this phase is the Request for Architecture
           Work.
      E.   One of the outputs of this phase is the Business Architecture.

Q7:   Which of the following statements about Phase E is true?
      A.   A key step in Phase E is to update the Technology Architecture.
      B.   A key step in Phase E is to brainstorm co-existence and
           interoperability requirements.
      C.   A key step in Phase E is to perform a requirements analysis.
      D.   One of the outputs from this phase is a trade-off analysis.
      E.   One of the outputs from this phase is a list of re-usable
           Architecture Building Blocks.

11.9 Recommended Reading

The following are recommended sources of further information for this chapter:

- TOGAF 8.1.1 Enterprise Edition Part II: ADM, Phase E: Opportunities and Solutions
- TOGAF 8.1.1 Enterprise Edition Part II: ADM, ADM Input and Output Descriptions

Chapter 12

Phase F: Migration Planning

12.1 Key Learning Points

This chapter describes Phase F: Migration Planning of the TOGAF
Architecture Development Method (ADM).

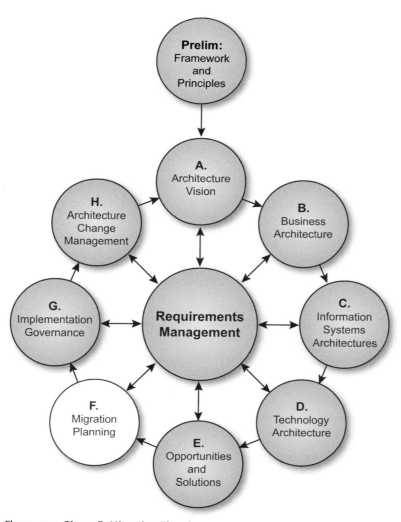

Figure 12.1: Phase F: Migration Planning

Key Points Explained

This chapter will help you to answer the following questions:

- What are the objectives of Phase F?
- What does Phase F consist of?
- What is its relationship to the rest of the TOGAF ADM?
- What are the inputs needed for Phase F?
- What are the outputs from Phase F?

12.2 Objectives

The objective of Phase F is to sort the various implementation projects into priority. Activities include assessing the dependencies, costs, and benefits of the various migration projects. The prioritized list of projects will form the basis of the detailed Implementation and Migration Plans.

12.3 Approach

The following list of questions can help when assessing the priorities of projects:

1. What are the implications of this project on other projects and activities?
2. What are the dependencies between this project and other projects and activities?
3. What products are needed?
4. What components must be developed?
5. Does the organization have the resources needed to develop such components?
6. What standards are the products or components built on?
7. When will they be available?
8. Will the products stand the test of time, considering the technology and the supplier's viability?
9. What is the cost of retraining users?
10. What is the likely cultural impact on the user community and how can it be controlled?
11. What is the total cost of the migration and what benefits will it deliver? Is funding available?
12. Is the migration viable?

Issues requiring consideration may include:

- Sequential *versus* parallel implementation of projects
- Choices of proceeding with phased migration by subsystem or by function
- The impact of geographical separation on migration

The decisions made should be incorporated in the Implementation Plan.

One approach is to implement business functions in a data-driven chronological sequence; i.e., develop or procure the applications and supporting technology that create data before those that process it and before those that store, archive, or delete data.

Example 12.1: An Approach to Implementing Systems in Data-Driven Chronological Sequence

(This example is taken from SPE 68794, Implementing Enterprise Architecture – Putting Quality Information in the Hands of Oil and Gas Knowledge Workers.)

1. Determine the future disposition of current systems. Business people, not IT people, should make these decisions. Each current system should be classified in one of the following categories:
   - A *mainstream system* categorized as part of the future information system
   - A *contain system* categorized as a system expected to be replaced or modified within the next three years
   - A *replace system* categorized to be replaced in the next three years
2. Applications should be combined or split into parts to facilitate sequencing and implementation. This rearrangement of applications creates a number of projects, a project being equivalent to an application or to combinations or parts of applications.
3. Develop the data sequence for the projects as described in the Data Architecture. Using the CRUD (Create/Read/Update/Delete) matrix developed as part of the Data Architecture, sequence the projects such that projects that create data precede projects that read or update that data.
4. Develop an estimated value to the business for each project. To do this, first develop a matrix based on a value index dimension and a risk index dimension. The value index includes the following criteria: principles compliance, which includes financial contribution, strategic alignment, and competitive position. The risk index includes the following criteria: size and complexity, technology, organizational capacity, and impact of a failure. Each of the criteria has an individual weight. The index and its criteria and weighting are developed and approved by senior management early in the project. It is important to establish the decision-making criteria before the options are known.

In addition, the following key business drivers may dictate the sequence of implementation:
- Cost reduction
- Service consolidation
- Ability to handle change
- Limiting the number of interim solutions

12.4 Inputs

The inputs to this phase are:
- Request for Architecture Work
- Statement of Architecture Work
- Target Business Architecture, Version 1.0
- Target Technology Architecture, Version 1.0
- Target Data Architecture, Version 1.0
- Target Applications Architecture, Version 1.0
- Impact Analysis – project list

12.5 Steps

12.5.1 Prioritize Projects
(Syllabus reference: 1.F.1)

The first step in this phase is to prioritize the migration projects identified in the Impact Analysis project list produced in Phase E (see Section 15.2.23).

12.5.2 Resourcing
(Syllabus reference: 1.F.2)

For each of the projects an estimate should be made of the resource requirements and availability of resources.

12.5.3 Cost/Benefit Assessment
(Syllabus reference: 1.F.3)

For each of the projects a cost/benefit assessment should be made. This will identify the projects most likely to make the most impact in proportion to their cost.

12.5.4 Risk Assessment
(Syllabus reference: 1.F.4)

For each of the projects a risk assessment should be performed. This should identify any high-risk projects.

12.5.5 Implementation Roadmap
(Syllabus reference: 1.F.5)

A proposed implementation roadmap should then be generated taking into account information learned in the previous steps of this phase. This roadmap should include a schedule for implementation.

12.5.6 Migration Plan
(Syllabus reference: 1.F.6)

A Migration Plan should then be prepared documenting how the existing systems will migrate to the new architecture (see Section 15.2.24).

12.6 Outputs
The outputs of this phase are:
- Impact Analysis – detailed Implementation Plan and Migration Plan (including Architecture Implementation Contract)

12.7 Summary
Phase G addresses migration planning; that is, how to move from the Baseline to the Target Architectures. It includes work prioritization, selection of the major work packages, and development of a Migration Plan.

12.8 Test Yourself Questions

Q1:   Which of the following questions does TOGAF recommend be asked
        when assessing priorities of projects?
        A.   What components need to be developed?
        B.   What are the costs of retraining users?
        C.   What are the benefits of the migration?
        D.   Does the organization have the resources to develop the
             components?
        E.   All of these

Q2:   Decisions made when assessing the priorities of projects should be
        incorporated into the:
        A.   Gap Analysis
        B.   Statement of Architecture Work
        C.   Baseline Technology Architecture
        D.   Implementation Plan
        E.   Target Technology Architecture

Q3:   When implementing business functions in a data-driven chronological
        sequence, what categorization is made for current systems that are part
        of the future information system?
        A.   Replace systems
        B.   Mainstream systems
        C.   Mainframe systems
        D.   Contain systems
        E.   Legacy systems

Q4:   Which artifact of the Data Architecture part of Phase C should be used
        for sequencing projects in a data-driven chronological sequence?
        A.   The CRUD matrix
        B.   Gap analysis
        C.   Impact Analysis
        D.   Statement of Architecture Work
        E.   Data principles

Q5: When preparing the detailed Migration Plan, which of the following should not be a consideration?

A. Risk assessment
B. Project priorities
C. Availability of resources
D. Cost/benefit assessment
E. Choice of target platform

12.9 Recommended Reading

The following are recommended sources of further information for this chapter:

- TOGAF 8.1.1 Enterprise Edition Part II: ADM, Phase F: Migration Planning
- TOGAF 8.1.1 Enterprise Edition Part II: ADM, ADM Input and Output Descriptions

Chapter 13

Phase G: Implementation Governance

13.1 Key Learning Points

This chapter describes Phase G: Implementation Governance of the TOGAF
Architecture Development Method (ADM).

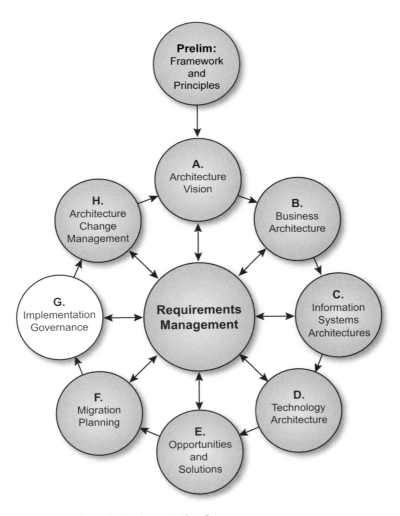

Figure 13.1: Phase G: Implementation Governance

Key Points Explained

This chapter will help you to answer the following questions:

- What are the objectives of Phase G?
- What does Phase G consist of?
- What is its relationship to the rest of the TOGAF ADM?
- What are the inputs needed for Phase G?
- What are the outputs from Phase G?

13.2 Objectives

The objectives of Phase G are to:

- Formulate recommendations for each implementation project
- Construct an Architecture Contract to govern the overall implementation and deployment process
- Perform appropriate governance functions while the system is being implemented and deployed
- Ensure conformance with the defined architecture by implementation projects and other projects

13.3 Approach

Phase G establishes the connection between the architecture and the implementation through the Architecture Contract (see Section 15.2.26). All the information for successful management of the various implementation projects must be brought together here. The actual development happens in parallel with Phase G. Project details are developed, including:

- Name, description, and objectives
- Scope, deliverables, and constraints
- Measures of effectiveness
- Acceptance criteria
- Risks and issues

Implementation governance is closely allied to overall architecture governance (see Chapter 22). A key aspect is ensuring compliance with the defined architecture(s) by the implementation projects and any other ongoing projects (see TOGAF 8.1.1 Enterprise Edition Part IV: Resource Base, Architecture Compliance).

> **Architecture Governance**
>
> The Architecture Contract produced in this phase features prominently in the area of architecture governance (see Chapter 22). It is often used as the means to driving change. In order to ensure that the Architecture Contract is effective and efficient, the following aspects of the governance framework should be introduced in this phase:
> - Simple process
> - People-centered authority
> - Strong communication
> - Timely responses and effective escalation process
> - Supporting organization structures

13.4 Inputs

The inputs to this phase are:
- Request for Architecture Work
- Statement of Architecture Work
- Re-usable Solution Building Blocks (from the organization's Solutions Continuum
- Impact Analysis – detailed Implementation Plan and Migration Plan (including Architecture Implementation Contract)

13.5 Steps

13.5.1 Formulate Project Recommendations

(Syllabus reference: 1.G.1)

The first step is to formulate recommendations for each separate project identified in the Impact Analysis generated in the previous phase. For each project:
- Document the scope of the project
- Document strategic requirements (from the architecture perspective)
- Document change requests
- Document rules for conformance
- Document schedule from roadmap

13.5.2   Document Architecture Contract
(Syllabus reference: 1.G.2)

The next step is to obtain signatures from all developing organizations and sponsoring organizations. This is part of ensuring that the management of all the projects is brought together.

13.5.3   Ongoing Implementation Governance
(Syllabus reference: 1.G.3)

The final step in this phase is to establish ongoing implementation governance and a formal Architecture Compliance Review process (see Section 22.2).

13.6   Outputs
The outputs of this phase are:

- Impact Analysis – Implementation Recommendations (see Section 15.2.25)
- Architecture Contract
- The architecture-compliant implemented system

Architecture Contract

This is a signed statement of intent drawn up between the architecting function within the enterprise and the implementation organization that will subsequently be building and deploying systems in the architected environment (see Section 15.2.26 for more information).

13.7   Summary
Phase G: Implementation Governance defines architecture constraints on the implementation projects and constructs and obtains signatures on an Architecture Contract. The contract, along with all the documentation, is then delivered to the implementation team. The final step is to monitor the implementation work for conformance.

13.8 Test Yourself Questions

Q1:   Which of the following is not an objective of Phase G?
- A.   Formulate recommendations for each implementation project
- B.   Construct an Architecture Contract to govern the overall implementation and deployment process
- C.   Perform appropriate governance functions while the system is being implemented and deployed
- D.   Ensure that the architecture is able to respond to the needs of the business
- E.   Ensure conformance with the defined architecture by implementation projects and other projects

Q2:   TOGAF suggests, but does not require, the use of ... to provide a foundation for governing the implementation of the recommended projects:
- A.   Impact Analysis
- B.   Principles
- C.   Strategic Plan
- D.   Architecture Contracts
- E.   Risk Assessment

Q3:   TOGAF states that a parallel activity that takes place during Phase G is:
- A.   The actual implementation
- B.   Generation of a gap analysis report
- C.   Review of the Technical Architecture
- D.   Development of architecture principles
- E.   Development of an Architecture Vision statement

13.9 Recommended Reading

The following are recommended sources of further information for this chapter:
- TOGAF 8.1.1 Enterprise Edition Part II: ADM, Phase G: Implementation Governance
- TOGAF 8.1.1 Enterprise Edition Part II: ADM, ADM Input and Output Descriptions

- TOGAF 8.1.1 Enterprise Edition Part IV: Resource Base, Architecture Contracts
- TOGAF 8.1.1 Enterprise Edition Part IV: Resource Base, Architecture Governance

Chapter 14

Phase H: Architecture Change Management

14.1 Key Learning Points

This chapter describes Phase H: Architecture Change Management of the TOGAF Architecture Development Method (ADM).

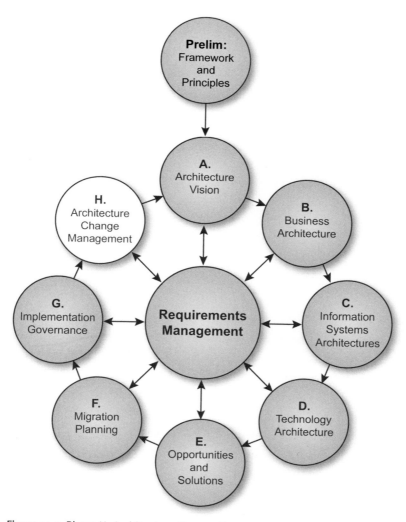

Figure 14.1: Phase H: Architecture Change Management

Key Points Explained

This chapter will help you to answer the following questions:

- What are the objectives of Phase H?
- What does Phase H consist of?
- What is its relationship to the rest of the TOGAF ADM?
- What are the inputs needed for Phase H?
- What are the outputs from Phase H?

14.2 Objectives

The objective of Phase H is to establish an architecture change management process. This will provide continual monitoring of changes in technology, business, etc. and also determine whether to initiate a new architecture cycle. Phase H also provides for changes to the framework and principles set up in the Preliminary Phase.

14.3 Approach

The goal of an architecture change management process is to ensure that changes to the architecture are managed properly and to support a dynamic architecture; i.e., one that has the flexibility to evolve rapidly in response to changes in technology and business. The process will determine:

- The circumstances under which the architecture will be permitted to change after implementation and the process for this
- The circumstances under which the ADM will be used again

The architecture change management process is very closely related to the architecture governance processes and the management of the Architecture Contract. It is critical that the governance body establish criteria to judge whether a change request warrants a new cycle of the ADM or just an architecture update. Such criteria are difficult to prescribe. It is particularly important to avoid "creeping elegance" and the governance body should look for changes that relate directly to business value.

14.3.1 Drivers for Architecture Change

Examples of technology-related drivers for change include:

- New technology reports
- Asset management cost reductions

- Technology withdrawal
- Standards initiatives

Business drivers for change include:
- Business-as-usual developments
- Business exceptions
- Business innovations
- Business technology innovations
- Strategic change

14.3.2 Change Management Process

The change management process involves determining how changes are to be managed, what techniques are to be applied, and what methodologies used. The process also determines which phases are impacted by requirements. Project management methods such as PRINCE 2, service management methods such as ITIL, management consultancy methods such as Catalyst, etc. can be used.

There are three main categories of architecture change:
1. **Simplification**: this can be handled via change management techniques. This may be a response to a request to reduce investment.
2. **Incremental**: this may be handled via change management techniques, or it may require partial re-architecting, depending on the nature of the change (see Section 14.3.3). This may be a response to a request to derive additional value from existing investment.
3. **Re-architecting**: this requires putting the whole architecture through the architecture development cycle again. This may be a response to a request to increase investment for exploitation.

To determine whether a change is simplification, incremental, or re-architecting, the following activities are undertaken:
1. Register all events that may impact the architecture
2. Allocate resources and management for the architecture tasks
3. The process or role responsible for resources has to make an assessment of what should be done
4. Evaluate the impact

> **PRINCE 2**
>
> PRINCE (Projects in Controlled Environments) is a project management method from the UK Office of Government Commerce (OGC). The latest version of the method, PRINCE 2, is designed to incorporate the requirements of existing users and to enhance the method towards a generic, best practice approach for the management of all types of projects; see www.ogc.gov.uk/prince2.
>
> **ITIL**
>
> The Information Technology Infrastructure Library (ITIL) also from the UK Office of Government Commerce consists of a series of books giving guidance on the provision of quality IT services, and on the accommodation and environmental facilities needed to support IT; see www.itil.co.uk for more information.

14.3.3 Guidelines for Maintenance versus Architecture Redesign

If the change:

- Impacts two stakeholders or more, then it is likely to require an architecture redesign and re-entry to the ADM
- Impacts only one stakeholder, then it is likely to be a candidate for change management
- Can be allowed under a dispensation, then it is likely to be a candidate for change management

Table 14-1 gives further examples of scenarios and the impact of change.

Table 14.1: Example Scenarios and Impact of Change

Scenario	Change Impact
The impact of the change is significant for the business strategy.	Architecture redesign needed since there may be a need to redo the whole enterprise architecture. This is thus a re-architecting change.
A new technology or standard emerges in a proposed change.	This would imply a refresh to the Technology Architecture but not the whole enterprise architecture and is thus an incremental change.
The change is at an infrastructure level; for example, ten systems reduced or changed to one system.	This may not change the architecture above the physical layer, but it will change the Baseline Description of the Technology Architecture. This would be a simplification change handled via change management techniques.

Scenario	Change Impact
The Foundation Architecture needs to be re- aligned with the business strategy. or: Substantial change is required to components and guidelines for use in deployment of the architecture. or: Significant standards used in the product architecture are changed which have significant end-user impact; e.g., regulatory changes.	A refreshment cycle (partial or complete re-architecting) may be required. If a refreshment cycle is needed, then a new Request for Architecture Work must be issued.

14.4 Inputs

The inputs to this phase are:

- Requests for Architecture Change due to technology changes (see Section 14.3.1)
- Requests for Architecture Change due to business changes (see Section 14.3.1)

14.5 Steps

The steps in this phase are ongoing and recur. They are driven by receipt of change requests.

14.5.1 Monitoring Technology Changes
(Syllabus reference: 1.H.1)

An ongoing activity of this phase is to monitor technology changes.

14.5.2 Monitoring Business Changes
(Syllabus reference: 1.H.2)

An ongoing activity of this phase is to monitor business changes.

14.5.3 Assessment of Changes
(Syllabus reference: 1.H.3)

When change requests are received, a process should be invoked to assess the change and to develop a proposed action for the change request.

14.5.4 Architecture Board Meeting
(Syllabus reference: 1.H.4)

A meeting of the Architecture Board (or other governing council) should then be convened to make decisions on the handling of all changes (technology and business).

14.6 Outputs
The outputs of this phase are:
- Architecture updates
- Changes to architecture framework and principles
- New Request for Architecture Work, to initiate another cycle of the ADM

14.7 Summary
Phase H: Change Management:
- Ensures that changes to the architecture are managed in a cohesive and controlled manner in line with the establish architecture governance processes
- Establishes and supports the enterprise architecture to provide flexibility to evolve the architecture rapidly in response to changes in the technology or business environment

14.8 Test Yourself Questions
Q1:   The primary goal of an architecture change management process is:
   A.   To ensure that business continues as usual
   B.   To determine whether a change warrants an update to the architecture
   C.   To determine whether a change requires a new cycle of the ADM

     D.   To manage change properly

     E.   To establish criteria for judging change requests

Q2:   What is a dynamic architecture?

     A.   One that is implemented in Java

     B.   One that can evolve in response to changes in technology and business

     C.   One that uses dynamic binding

     D.   One that has been documented using an ADL

     E.   One that uses object-oriented frameworks

Q3:   Which of the following is not a technology-related driver for architecture change?

     A.   Standards initiatives

     B.   Technology withdrawal

     C.   New technology reports

     D.   Strategic change

     E.   Asset management

Q4:   Which of the following is a key step in Phase H?

     A.   Monitoring of technology changes

     B.   Monitoring of business changes

     C.   Meetings of the Architecture Board

     D.   Assessment of changes

     E.   All of these

Q5:   If a refreshment cycle is required by a change, what is the immediate impact?

     A.   A refresh of the Technology Architecture is required.

     B.   A new Statement of Architecture Work is required.

     C.   A new Request for Architecture Work is required.

     D.   A refresh of the Migration Plan is required.

     E.   All of these

14.9 Recommended Reading

The following are recommended sources of further information for this chapter:

- TOGAF 8.1.1 Enterprise Edition Part II: ADM, Phase H: Change Management
- TOGAF 8.1.1 Enterprise Edition Part II: ADM, ADM Input and Output Descriptions
- TOGAF 8.1.1 Enterprise Edition Part IV: Resource Base, Architecture Board
- TOGAF 8.1.1 Enterprise Edition Part IV: Resource Base, Architecture Governance

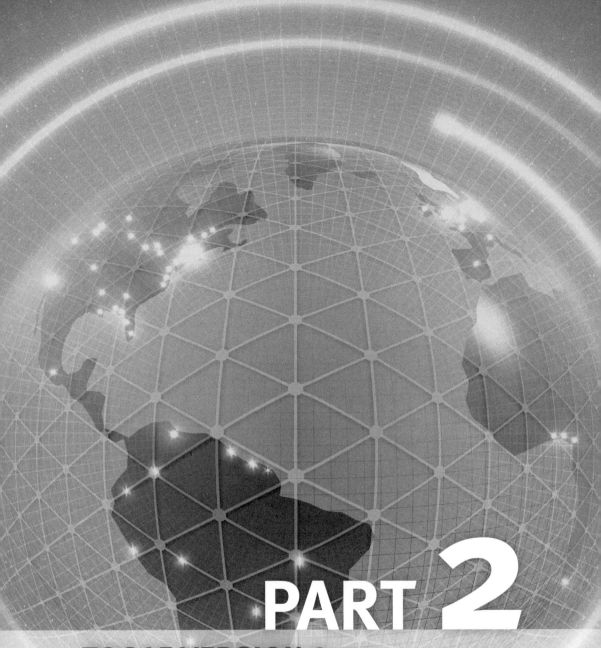

PART 2

TOGAF VERSION 8.1.1
Architecture Development
Method (ADM) Information Sets

Chapter 15

ADM Information Sets

15.1 Key Learning Points

This chapter provides descriptions of the Architecture Development Method (ADM) Information Sets and corresponds to Part 2 of the TOGAF 8 Certified Course Syllabus (see Appendix D).

This chapter will help you to understand the contents of key deliverables and processes of the ADM cycle. Table 15-1 gives a roadmap to this chapter by the ADM phase in which the deliverables and processes are used. For each point, key facts are presented and (if appropriate) references to other sections within this Study Guide and to the TOGAF 8.1.1 Enterprise Edition documentation are given.

Table 15.1: Roadmap to Chapter 15

ADM Phase	Reference(s)
Preliminary Phase: Framework & Principles	Section 15.2.1, Framework Definition Section 15.2.2, Architecture Principles Section 15.2.3, Business Principles, Goals, and Drivers Section 15.2.4, IT Governance Strategy
Phase A: Architecture Vision	Section 15.2.5, Request for Architecture Work Section 15.2.6, Statement of Architecture Work Section 15.2.7, Architecture Vision Section 15.2.19, Architecture Viewpoints Section 15.2.20, Architecture Views
Phase B: Business Architecture	Section 15.2.8, Business Architecture Section 15.2.9, Business Architecture Report Section 15.2.10, Business Requirements Section 15.2.11, Technical Requirements Section 15.2.12, Gap Analysis Section 15.2.19, Architecture Viewpoints Section 15.2.20, Architecture Views Section 15.2.21, Re-Usable Architecture Building Blocks Section 15.2.22, Re-Usable Solution Building Blocks

ADM Phase	Reference(s)
Phase C: Information Systems Architectures	Section 15.2.12, Gap Analysis Section 15.2.13, Data Architecture Section 15.2.14, Data Architecture Report Section 15.2.15, Applications Architecture Section 15.2.16, Applications Architecture Report Section 15.2.19, Architecture Viewpoints Section 15.2.20, Architecture Views Section 15.2.21, Re-Usable Architecture Building Blocks Section 15.2.22, Re-Usable Solution Building Blocks
Phase D: Technology Architecture	Section 15.2.12, Gap Analysis Section 15.2.17, Technology Architecture Section 15.2.18, Technology Architecture Report Section 15.2.19, Architecture Viewpoints Section 15.2.20, Architecture Views Section 15.2.21, Re-Usable Architecture Building Blocks Section 15.2.22, Re-Usable Solution Building Blocks
Phase E: Opportunities and Solutions	Section 15.2.21, Re-Usable Architecture Building Blocks Section 15.2.22, Re-Usable Solution Building Blocks Section 15.2.23, Impact Analysis Document – Project List Section 15.2.27, Product Information
Phase F: Migration Planning	Section 15.2.24, Impact Analysis Document – Migration Plan
Phase G: Implementation Governance	Section 15.2.25, Impact Analysis Document – Implementation Recommendations Section 15.2.26, Architecture Contracts
Phase H: Architecture Change Management	Section 15.2.28, Request for Architecture Change Section 15.2.29, New Technology Reports Section 15.2.30, Requirements Impact Statement

An architecture team should use TOGAF's breadth of tools to focus on completing well-scoped projects in short order by following the steps of the ADM cycle. With each iteration through the ADM, the architecture becomes better defined, and the effort required decreases as the architecture team gains experience.

Bill Estrem, "TOGAF to the Rescue" (www.opengroup.org/downloads)

15.2 Information Sets

15.2.1 Framework Definition
(Syllabus reference: 2.1)

Selecting and defining a framework is the practical starting point for an architecture project. Building on TOGAF has a number of advantages over creating a framework from scratch:
- It avoids the initial panic when the scale of the task becomes apparent.
- Use of TOGAF is systematic – "codified common sense".
- TOGAF captures what others have found to work in real life.
- TOGAF has a baseline set of resources to re-use.
- TOGAF defines a Foundation Architecture in the Enterprise Continuum.

SEE ALSO
Section 2.2.4; Section 2.2.5; Section 2.2.7; Chapter 3

15.2.2 Architecture Principles
(Syllabus reference: 2.2)

This set of documentation is an initial output of the Preliminary Phase. It is the set of general rules and guidelines for the architecture being developed. See TOGAF 8.1.1 Enterprise Edition Part IV: Resource Base, Architecture Principles for guidelines and a detailed set of generic architecture principles. The suggested contents of this document are business principles, data principles, applications principles, and technology principles.

15.2.2.1 Developing Architecture Principles
The Lead Architect, in conjunction with the enterprise CIO, Architecture Board, and other key business stakeholders, typically develops architecture principles; see Section 4.4.1.1 for a recommended template and two examples.

The following typically influences the development of architecture principles:
- Enterprise mission and plans: the mission, plans, and organizational infrastructure of the enterprise.
- Enterprise strategic initiatives: the characteristics of the enterprise – its strengths, weaknesses, opportunities, and threats – and its current

enterprise-wide initiatives (such as process improvement and quality management).

- External constraints: market factors (time-to-market imperatives, customer expectations, etc.); existing and potential legislation.
- Current systems and technology: the set of information resources deployed within the enterprise, including systems documentation, equipment inventories, network configuration diagrams, policies, and procedures.
- Computer industry trends: predictions about the usage, availability, and cost of computer and communication technologies, referenced from credible sources along with associated best practices presently in use.

15.2.2.2 Qualities of Principles

There are five criteria that distinguish a good set of principles, as shown in Table 15-2.

Table 15.2: Recommended Criteria for Quality Principles

Criteria	Description
Understandability	The underlying tenets of a principle can be quickly grasped and understood by individuals throughout the organization. The intention of the principle is clear and unambiguous, so that violations, whether intentional or not, are minimized.
Robustness	Principles should enable good quality decisions about architectures and plans to be made, and enforceable policies and standards to be created. Each principle should be sufficiently definitive and precise to support consistent decision-making in complex, potentially controversial situations.
Completeness	Every potentially important principle governing the management of information and technology for the organization is defined. The principles cover every situation perceived.
Consistency	Strict adherence to one principle may require a loose interpretation of another principle. The set of principles must be expressed in a way that allows a balance of interpretations. Principles should not be contradictory to the point where adhering to one principle would violate the spirit of another. Every word in a principle statement should be carefully chosen to allow consistent yet flexible interpretation.
Stability	Principles should be enduring, yet able to accommodate changes. An amendment process should be established for adding, removing, or altering principles after they are ratified initially.

15.2.2.3 Applying Architecture Principles

Architecture principles are used to capture the fundamental truths about how the enterprise will use and deploy IT resources and assets. The principles are used in a number of different ways:

1. To provide a framework within which the enterprise can start to make conscious decisions about IT

2. As a guide to establishing relevant evaluation criteria, thus exerting strong influence on the selection of products or product architectures in the later stages of managing compliance to the IT architecture

3. As drivers for defining the functional requirements of the architecture

4. As an input to assessing both existing IS/IT systems and the future strategic portfolio, for compliance with the defined architectures; these assessments will provide valuable insights into the transition activities needed to implement an architecture, in support of business goals and priorities

5. The Rationale statements (see below) highlight the value of the architecture to the enterprise, and therefore provide a basis for justifying architecture activities

6. The Implications statements (see below) provide an outline of the key tasks, resources, and potential costs to the enterprise of following the principle; they also provide valuable inputs to future transition initiatives and planning activities

7. To support the architecture governance activities in terms of:
   — Providing a "back-stop" for the standard Architecture Compliance assessments where some interpretation is allowed or required
   — Supporting a decision to initiate a dispensation request where the implications of a particular architecture amendment cannot be resolved within local operating procedure

Principles are inter-related, and need to be applied as a set. Principles will sometimes compete; for example, the principles of "accessibility" and "security". Each principle must be considered in the context of "all other things being equal". At times a decision will be required as to which principle will take precedence on a particular issue. The rationale for such decisions should always be documented. The fact that a principle seems self-evident does not mean that the principle is actually observed in an organization, even when there are verbal acknowledgements of the principle. Although specific penalties are not prescribed in a declaration of principles, violations of principles generally cause operational problems and inhibit the ability of the organization to fulfill its mission.

SEE ALSO
Section 4.4.1.1; TOGAF 8.1.1 Enterprise Edition Part IV: Resource Base, Architecture Principles

15.2.3 Business Principles, Goals, and Drivers
(Syllabus reference: 2.3)

A statement of the business principles, goals, and drivers has usually been defined elsewhere in the enterprise prior to the architecture activity. They are restated as an output of the Preliminary Phase and reviewed again as a part of Phase A: Architecture Vision. The activity in Phase A is to ensure that the current definitions are correct and clear. The TOGAF Resource Base (TOGAF 8.1.1 Enterprise Edition Part IV: Resource Base) contains an example set of eight business principles that are a useful starting point.

SEE ALSO
Section 5.4.2; TOGAF 8.1.1 Enterprise Edition Part IV: Resource Base, Architecture Principles

15.2.4 IT Governance Strategy
(Syllabus reference: 2.4)

An IT governance strategy, and an appropriate organization for implementing the strategy, must be established with the backing of top management, clarifying who owns the enterprise's IT resources, and, in particular, who has ultimate responsibility for their enterprise-wide integration. IT governance is a broad topic and outside of the scope of the TOGAF document. TOGAF recommends COBIT as a source for further information.

COBIT
The Control Objectives for Information and related Technology (COBIT) created by the Information Systems Audit and Control Association (ISACA) and the IT Governance Institute (ITGI) is an example of an IT governance framework. It is a set of best practices (framework) for developing appropriate IT governance and control in a company (see www.isaca.org/cobit).

SEE ALSO

Section 4.4.2; Section 22.2; TOGAF 8.1.1 Enterprise Edition Part IV: Resource Base, Architecture Governance

15.2.5 Request for Architecture Work
(Syllabus reference: 2.5)

This is a document that is sent from the sponsoring organization to the architecture organization. Often it is produced with the assistance of the architecture organization. It is an input to Phase A: Architecture Vision. In general all the information in this document should be at a high level. The suggested contents of this document are as follows:

- Organization sponsors
- Organization's mission statement
- Business goals (and changes)
- Strategic plans of the business
- Time limits
- Changes in the business environment
- Organizational constraints
- Budget information, financial constraints
- External constraints, business constraints
- Current business system description
- Current architecture/IT system description
- Description of developing organization
- Description of resources available to developing organization

SEE ALSO

Section 5.3; TOGAF 8.1.1 Enterprise Edition Part II: ADM, ADM Input and Output Descriptions

15.2.6 Statement of Architecture Work
(Syllabus reference: 2.6)

The Statement of Architecture Work is created as a deliverable of Phase A, and is effectively a contract between the architecting organization and the sponsor of the architecture project. This document is a response to the Request for Architecture Work input document (see Section 15.2.5). It should describe an overall plan to address the request for work and propose how solutions to the problems that have been identified will be addressed through the architecture process. The suggested contents of this document are as follows:

- Statement of work title
- Project request and background
- Project description and scope
- Architecture Vision
- Managerial approach
- Change of scope procedures
- Responsibilities and deliverables
- Acceptance criteria and procedures
- Project plan and schedule
- Support of the Enterprise Continuum (re-use)
- Signature approvals

15.2.7 Architecture Vision
(Syllabus reference: 2.7)

A key step in Phase A is to identify key stakeholders and their concerns; define key business requirements and articulate an Architecture Vision to address them, within the scope and constraints, whilst conforming to business and architecture principles. Business scenarios are an appropriate and important technique that can be used as part of the process in developing an Architecture Vision document. Note that they can be used at various stages of the ADM. They are a method for ensuring that the enterprise architecture being produced is linked to business requirements. See TOGAF 8.1.1 Enterprise Edition Part IV: Resource Base, Business Scenarios for further information. The suggested contents are as follows:

- Problem description:
  — Purpose of scenario
- Detailed objectives
- Environment and process models:
  — Process description
  — Process steps mapped to environment
  — Process steps mapped to people
  — Information flow
- Actors and their roles and responsibilities:
  — Human actors and roles

— Computer actors and roles
— Requirements
- Resulting architecture model:
  — Constraints
  — IT principles
  — Architecture supporting the process
  — Requirements mapped to architecture

SEE ALSO

Section 5.4.6; TOGAF 8.1.1 Enterprise Edition Part IV: Resource Base, Business Scenarios

15.2.8 Business Architecture
(Syllabus reference: 2.8)

The objective of Phase B is to develop the Business Architecture. The topics that should be addressed in the Business Architecture are as follows:
- Baseline Business Architecture: this is a description of the existing Business Architecture (Baseline Business Architecture); see Section 6.5.1.
- Business goals, objectives, and constraints:
  — Business requirements and key system and architecture drivers
  — Business return given required changes
  — Assumptions (e.g., business, financial, organizational, or required technical functionality)
  — Business Architecture principles
- Business Architecture models (see Section 6.5.3):
  — Organization structure
  — Business functions
  — Business roles
  — Correlation of organization and functions
  — Business Architecture Building Blocks list (e.g., business services)
  — Business Architecture Building Blocks models
  — Candidate Solution Building Blocks list
  — Candidate Solution Building Blocks models
  — Relevant business process descriptions, including measures and deliverables
- Technical requirements (drivers for other architecture work)

15.2.9 Business Architecture Report
(Syllabus reference: 2.9)

The Business Architecture Report, produced in Phase B, is a log of the architecture activity undertaken in the phase, and rationale for any key decisions.

15.2.10 Business Requirements
(Syllabus reference: 2.10)

The business scenarios technique is used to discover and document business requirements.

SEE ALSO
Chapter 6; TOGAF 8.1.1 Enterprise Edition Part II: ADM, Phase B: Business Architecture; TOGAF 8.1.1 Enterprise Edition Part IV: Resource Base, Business Scenarios

15.2.11 Technical Requirements
(Syllabus reference: 2.11)

An initial set of technical requirements should be generated as the output of Phase B: Business Architecture. These are the drivers for the Technology Architecture work that follows, and should identify, categorize, and prioritize the implications for work in the remaining architecture domains.

SEE ALSO
Chapter 6; TOGAF 8.1.1 Enterprise Edition Part II: ADM, Phase B: Business Architecture

15.2.12 Gap Analysis
(Syllabus reference: 2.12)

The technique known as gap analysis is widely used in the TOGAF ADM to validate an architecture that is being developed. It is usually the final step within a phase. The basic premise is to highlight a shortfall between the Baseline Architecture and the Target Architecture; that is, items that have been deliberately omitted, accidentally left out, or not yet defined.

The steps are as follows:

- Draw up a matrix with all the Architecture Building Blocks (ABBs) of the Baseline Architecture on the vertical axis, and all the ABBs of the Target Architecture on the horizontal axis.
- Add to the Baseline Architecture axis a final row labeled "New ABBs", and to the Target Architecture axis a final column labeled "Eliminated ABBs".
- Where an ABB is available in both the Baseline and Target Architectures, record this with "Included" at the intersecting cell.
- Where an ABB from the Baseline Architecture is missing in the Target Architecture, each must be reviewed. If it was correctly eliminated, mark it as such in the appropriate "Eliminated" cell. If it was not, you have uncovered an accidental omission in your Target Architecture that must be addressed by reinstating the ABB in the next iteration of the architecture design – mark it as such in the appropriate "Eliminated" cell.
- Where an ABB from the Target Architecture cannot be found in the Baseline Architecture, mark it at the intersection with the "New" row as a gap that needs to filled, either by developing or procuring the building block.

When the exercise is complete, anything under "Eliminated Services" or "New Services" is a gap, which should either be explained as correctly eliminated, or marked as to be addressed by reinstating or developing/procuring the function.

Figure 15-1 shows examples of gaps between the Baseline Architecture and the Target Architecture; in this case the missing elements are "broadcast services" and "shared screen services".

The phases where it is recommended that the gap analysis technique be used in the ADM are shown in Table 15-3.

Target Architecture → Baseline Architecture ↓	Video Conferencing Services	Enhanced Telephony Services	Mailing List Services	Eliminated Services ↓
Broadcast Services				Intentionally Eliminated
Video Conferencing Services	Included			
Enhanced Telephony Services		Potential Match		
Shared Screen Services				Unintentionally excluded – a gap in Target Architecture
New →		Gap: Enhanced services to be developed or produced	Gap: Enhanced services to be developed or produced	

Figure 15.1: Gap Analysis Example

Table 15.3: ADM Phases where Gap Analysis is used

ADM Phase	Reference
Phase B: Business Architecture	Section 6.5.8
Phase C: Information Systems Architectures – Data Architecture	Section 8.4.9
Phase C: Information Systems Architectures – Application Systems Architecture	Section 9.4.8
Phase D: Technology Architecture	Section 10.5.8

15.2.13 Data Architecture
(Syllabus reference: 2.13)

The objectives of Phase C are to produce the Data Architecture. It should comprise some or all of:
- Business data model
- Logical data model
- Data management process model
- Data entity/business function matrix
- Data interoperability requirements

SEE ALSO
Chapter 8

15.2.14 Data Architecture Report
(Syllabus reference: 2.14)

The Data Architecture Report produced in the Data Architecture part of Phase C summarizes the activities of the phase and the key findings (essentially providing a log of the activities in this phase).

15.2.15 Applications Architecture
(Syllabus reference: 2.15)

The Applications Architecture is developed as part of Phase C.

See Section 9.4.1 for a description of what should be defined as the Baseline Architecture description for each application. See Section 9.4.4 for a description of what should be defined for all candidate applications within the Target Architecture.

SEE ALSO
Chapter 9

15.2.16 Applications Architecture Report
(Syllabus reference: 2.16)

This is an output of the Applications Architecture part of Phase C. This should include a summary of the tasks undertaken in this phase and the key recommendations.

SEE ALSO
Chapter 9

15.2.17 Technology Architecture
(Syllabus reference: 2.17)

The Technology Architecture is developed in Phase D. The topics that should be addressed in the Technology Architecture are as follows:
- Baseline Technology Architecture
- Objectives and constraints:
  — Technology requirements and key system and architecture drivers
  — Assumptions (e.g., business, financial, organizational, or required technical functionality)
- Technology Architecture model(s):
  — Architecture Building Block (ABB) models of views (minimally a model of functions and a model of services)
  — ABB models of service portfolios (enterprise-specific framework)
- Technology Architecture specification:
  For each ABB produce:
  — Details of the technical functionality
  — A fully defined list of all the standards
  — A description of the building blocks at the levels necessary to support implementation, enterprise-wide strategic decision-making, and further iterations of the architecture definition process
  — Rationale for decisions taken that relate to the building block, including rationales for decisions not to do something
  — A specification for the building block identifying the interworking with other building blocks, including how
  — Guidelines for procuring
  — Standards summary list
- Requirements traceability

- Acceptance criteria:
  — Criteria for choosing specifications
  — Criteria for selection of portfolios of specifications
  — Criteria to test merits of architecture (key question list)
  — Report on cost/benefit analyses
  — Report on how the proposed architecture meets the business goals and objectives
  — Criteria response answers to key question list to test merits of architecture
- Gap report:
  — Report on gap analysis
  — Report of gap analysis matrix
- Mapping of the architectures in the Enterprise Continuum
- Change requests for extensions or amendments to related architectures

SEE ALSO
Chapter 10

15.2.18 Technology Architecture Report
(Syllabus reference: 2.18)

The Technology Architecture Report is produced as an output of Phase D: Technology Architecture. This should include a summary of the tasks undertaken in this phase and the key recommendations.

SEE ALSO
Chapter 10

15.2.19 Architecture Viewpoints
(Syllabus reference: 2.19)

The architect uses views and viewpoints in the ADM cycle during Phases A through to D for developing architectures for each domain (business, data, applications, technology). A "view" is what you see. A "viewpoint" is where you are looking from; the vantage point or perspective that determines what you see (a viewpoint can also be thought of as a schema). Viewpoints are generic, and can be stored in libraries for re-use. A view is always specific to the architecture for which it is created. Every view has an associated viewpoint that describes it, at least implicitly.

ANSI/IEEE Std 1471-2000 encourages architects to define viewpoints explicitly. Making this distinction between the content and schema of a view may seem at first to be an unnecessary overhead, but it provides a mechanism for re-using viewpoints across different architectures.

To illustrate the concepts of views and viewpoints, consider Example 15-1 that is a very simple airport system with two different stakeholders: the pilot and the air traffic controller.

Example 15.1: Views and Viewpoints for a Simple Airport System

Views and Viewpoints for a Simple Airport System
The pilot has one view of the system, and the air traffic controller has another. Neither view represents the whole system, because the perspective of each stakeholder constrains (and reduces) how each sees the overall system.
The view of the pilot comprises some elements not viewed by the controller, such as passengers and fuel, while the view of the controller comprises some elements not viewed by the pilot, such as other planes. There are also elements shared between the views, such as the communication model between the pilot and the controller, and the vital information about the plane itself.
A viewpoint is a model (or description) of the information contained in a view. In this example, one viewpoint is the description of how the pilot sees the system, and the other viewpoint is how the controller sees the system. Pilots describe the system from their perspective, using a model of their position and vector toward or away from the runway. All pilots use this model, and the model has a specific language that is used to capture information and populate the model. Controllers describe the system differently, using a model of the airspace and the locations and vectors of aircraft within the airspace. Again, all controllers use a common language derived from the common model in order to capture and communicate information pertinent to their viewpoint. Fortunately, when controllers talk with pilots, they use a common communication language. (In other words, the models representing their individual viewpoints partially intersect.) Part of this common language is about location and vectors of aircraft, and is essential to safety. So in essence each viewpoint is an abstract model of how all the stakeholders of a particular type – all pilots, or all controllers – view the airport system. The interface to the human user of a tool is typically close to the model and language associated with the viewpoint. The unique tools of the pilot are fuel, altitude, speed, and location indicators. The main tool of the controller is radar. The common tool is a radio.

To summarize from Example 15-1, we can see that a view can subset the system through the perspective of the stakeholder, such as the pilot *versus* the controller. This subset can be described by an abstract model called a viewpoint, such as an air flight *versus* an air space model. This description of the view is documented in a partially specialized language, such as "pilot-speak" *versus* "controller-speak". Tools are used to assist the stakeholders, and they interface with each other in terms of the language derived from the viewpoint. When stakeholders use common tools, such as the radio contact between pilot and controller, a common language is essential.

SEE ALSO

Section 15.2.20

15.2.20 Architecture Views

(Syllabus reference: 2.20)

Architecture views are representations of the overall architecture that are meaningful to one or more stakeholders in the system. The architect chooses and develops a set of views in the ADM cycle during Phases A through to D that enable the architecture to be communicated to, and understood by, all the stakeholders, and enable them to verify that the system will address their concerns. The concepts in Table 15-4 are central to the use of architecture views within TOGAF.

Table 15.4: The Concepts related to Architecture Views

Concept	Definition
System	A *system* is a collection of components organized to accomplish a specific function or set of functions.
Architecture	The *architecture* of a system is the system's fundamental organization, embodied in its components, their relationships to each other and to the environment, and the principles guiding its design and evolution.
Architecture Description	An *architecture description* is a collection of artifacts that document an architecture. In TOGAF, architecture views are the key artifacts in an architecture description.

Concept	Definition
Stakeholders	*Stakeholders* are people who have key roles in, or concerns about, the system; for example, as users, developers, or managers. Different stakeholders with different roles in the system will have different concerns. Stakeholders can be individuals, teams, or organizations (or classes thereof).
Concerns	*Concerns* are the key interests that are crucially important to the stakeholders in the system, and determine the acceptability of the system. Concerns may pertain to any aspect of the system's functioning, development, or operation, including considerations such as performance, reliability, security, distribution, and evolvability.
View	A *view* is a representation of a whole system from the perspective of a related set of concerns. In capturing or representing the design of a system's architecture, the architect will typically create one or more architecture models, possibly using different tools. A view will comprise selected parts of one or more models, chosen so as to demonstrate to a particular stakeholder or group of stakeholders that their concerns are being adequately addressed in the design of the system architecture.
Viewpoint	A *viewpoint* defines the perspective from which a view is taken. More specifically, a viewpoint defines: how to construct and use a view (by means of an appropriate schema or template); the information that should appear in the view; the modeling techniques for expressing and analyzing the information; and a rationale for these choices (e.g., by describing the purpose and intended audience of the view).

15.2.20.1 Developing Views in the ADM

The choice of which particular architecture views to develop is one of the key decisions that the architect has to make.

The architect has a responsibility for ensuring the completeness (fitness-for-purpose) of the architecture, in terms of adequately addressing all the pertinent concerns of its stakeholders; and the integrity of the architecture, in terms of connecting all the various views to each other, satisfactorily reconciling the conflicting concerns of different stakeholders, and showing the trade-offs made in so doing (as between security and performance, for example).

SEE ALSO

Section 15.2.19; TOGAF 8.1.1 Enterprise Edition Part IV: Resource Base, Developing Architecture Views

15.2.21 Re-Usable Architecture Building Blocks
(Syllabus reference: 2.21)

Re-usable Architecture Building Blocks (ABBs) are architecture documentation and models from the enterprise's Architecture Continuum (see Chapter 19). They are defined or selected during application of the ADM (mainly in Phases A, B, C, and D). The characteristics of ABBs are as follows:
- They define what functionality will be implemented
- They capture business and technical requirements
- They are technology-aware
- They direct and guide the development of Solution Building Blocks (see Section 15.2.22)

The content of ABB specifications includes the following as a minimum:
- Fundamental functionality and attributes: semantics, unambiguous, including security capability and manageability
- Interfaces: chosen set, supplied (APIs, data formats, protocols, hardware interfaces, standards)
- Dependent building blocks with required functionality and named user interfaces
- Map to business/organizational entities and policies

Each ABB should include a statement of any architecture documentation and models from the enterprise's Architecture Continuum that can be re-used in the architecture development. The specification of building blocks using the ADM is an evolutionary and iterative process. The key phases and steps of the ADM at which building blocks are evolved and specified are summarized below, and illustrated in Figure 15-2.

In Phase A, the earliest building block definitions start as relatively abstract entities within the Architecture Vision.

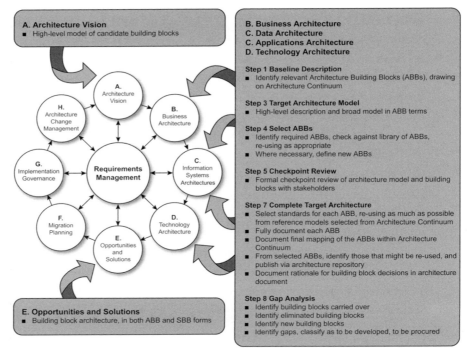

A. Architecture Vision
■ High-level model of candidate building blocks

B. Business Architecture
C. Data Architecture
C. Applications Architecture
D. Technology Architecture

Step 1 Baseline Description
■ Identify relevant Architecture Building Blocks (ABBs), drawing on Architecture Continuum

Step 3 Target Architecture Model
■ High-level description and broad model in ABB terms

Step 4 Select ABBs
■ Identify required ABBs, check against library of ABBs, re-using as appropriate
■ Where necessary, define new ABBs

Step 5 Checkpoint Review
■ Formal checkpoint review of architecture model and building blocks with stakeholders

Step 7 Complete Target Architecture
■ Select standards for each ABB, re-using as much as possible from reference models selected from Architecture Continuum
■ Fully document each ABB
■ Document final mapping of the ABBs within Architecture Continuum
■ From selected ABBs, identify those that might be re-used, and publish via architecture repository
■ Document rationale for building block decisions in architecture document

Step 8 Gap Analysis
■ Identify building blocks carried over
■ Identify eliminated building blocks
■ Identify new building blocks
■ Identify gaps, classify as to be developed, to be procured

E. Opportunities and Solutions
■ Building block architecture, in both ABB and SBB forms

Figure 15.2: Architecture Building Blocks and their use in the ADM Cycle

In Phases B, C, and D building blocks within the Business, Data, Applications, and Technology Architectures are evolved to a common pattern of steps:

- Step 1: Baseline Description produces a list of candidate building blocks, from the analysis of the baseline.
- Step 3: Target Architecture Model takes this list and high-level model as inputs, and evolves them iteratively into a definition of the Target Architecture, specified in terms of ABBs. Step 3 produces a high-level description and broad model of the target system in terms of ABBs and a rationale for each building block decision.
- Step 4: Select ABBs produces for each ABB a service description portfolio, built up as a set of non-conflicting services.
- Step 5: Checkpoint Review of the business goals and objectives produces confirmation of the merit and completeness of the model and service description portfolio, and a description of how the emerging Target Architecture meets the objectives of the architecture development.

- Step 7: Complete the Target Architecture fully specified in terms of ABBs, a fully defined (by service) list of all the standards that make up the Target Architecture, and all the ABBs that will be used to implement it, and a diagrammatic depiction of the building blocks at the levels needed to describe the strategic and implementation aspects of the architecture.
- Step 8: Gap Analysis produces a gap analysis report of the eliminated building blocks, carried over building blocks, and new building blocks.

Finally, in Phase E the building blocks become more implementation-specific as SBBs, and their interfaces become the detailed architecture specification. The output of Phase E is the building block architecture, both in ABB (i.e., functionally defined) and SBB (i.e., product-specific) forms.

SEE ALSO
TOGAF 8.1.1 Enterprise Edition Part IV: Resource Base, Building Blocks

15.2.22   Re-Usable Solution Building Blocks
(Syllabus reference: 2.22)

Re-usable Solution Building Blocks (SBBs) relate to the Solutions Continuum (see Chapter 20). They are implementations of the architectures identified in the enterprise's Architecture Continuum and may be either procured or developed. As noted in Section 15.2.21, SBBs appear in Phase E of the ADM where product-specific building blocks are considered for the first time. SBBs define what products and components will implement the functionality, thereby defining the implementation. They fulfill business requirements and are product or vendor-aware. The content of an SBB specification includes the following as a minimum:
- Specific functionality and attributes
- Interfaces; the implemented set
- Required SBBs used with required functionality and names of the interfaces used
- Mapping from the SBBs to the IT topology and operational policies
- Specifications of attributes shared such as security, manageability, localizability, scalability
- Performance, configurability
- Design drivers and constraints, including the physical architecture
- Relationships between the SBBs and ABBs

SEE ALSO
TOGAF 8.1.1 Enterprise Edition Part IV: Resource Base, Building Blocks

15.2.23 Impact Analysis Document – Project List
(Syllabus reference: 2.23)

The Impact Analysis document is a document generated in Phases E, F, and
G. Each phase updates the document. Phase E: Opportunities and Solutions
(see Chapter 11) adds the project list to the Impact Analysis document. It
identifies possible work packages or projects, together with classifications
and priorities. The recommended contents for the project list include the
name, description, and objectives of each impacted project, together with a
prioritized list of impacted projects to implement the proposed architecture.

SEE ALSO
Section 11.5.6

15.2.24 Impact Analysis Document – Migration Plan
(Syllabus reference: 2.24)

Phase F: Migration Planning (see Chapter 12) adds the Migration Plan to
the Impact Analysis document. This documents how existing systems will be
migrated to the new architecture. The recommended contents for a Migration
Plan should address the benefits of migration (including mapping to business
requirements), together with the estimated costs of the migration options.

SEE ALSO
Section 12.5.6

15.2.25 Impact Analysis Document – Implementation Recommendations
Phase G: Implementation Governance (see Chapter 13) adds the
implementation recommendations to the Impact Analysis document. The
recommended contents for Implementation Recommendations should
include criteria measures for the effectiveness of the projects, identified risks
and issues, and a description and model of the Solution Building Blocks.

SEE ALSO

Section 13.6

15.2.26 Architecture Contracts

Architecture Contracts are produced in Phase G: Implementation Governance (see Chapter 13). Typical contents of an Architecture Design and Development Contract are:

- Introduction and background
- The nature of the agreement
- Scope of the architecture
- Architecture and strategic principles and requirements
- Conformance requirements
- Architecture development and management process and roles
- Target architecture measures
- Defined phases of deliverables
- Prioritized joint workplan
- Time window(s)
- Architecture delivery and business metrics

Typical contents of a Business Users' Architecture Contract produced in Phase G are:

- Introduction and background
- The nature of the agreement
- Scope
- Strategic requirements
- Conformance requirements
- Architecture adopters
- Time window
- Architecture business metrics
- Service architecture (includes Service Level Agreement (SLA))

This contract is also used to manage changes to the enterprise architecture in Phase H (see Chapter 14).

SEE ALSO

Section 13.5.2; TOGAF 8.1.1 Enterprise Edition Part IV: Resource Base, Architecture Contracts

15.2.27 Product Information

(Syllabus reference: 2.27)

Product information is an input to Phase E: Opportunities and Solutions. Where there are product implementations that are candidates for the architecture implementation, then a document should be produced containing functional descriptions of the candidate products, together with architecture descriptions of the candidate elements.

SEE ALSO

Chapter 11

15.2.28 Request for Architecture Change

(Syllabus reference: 2.28)

According to Phase H, Requests for Architecture Change are driven by technology changes or business changes. TOGAF provides a set of guidelines for reviewing Requests for Architecture Change to enable a controlled and consistent change management process.

SEE ALSO

Chapter 14

15.2.29 New Technology Reports

(Syllabus reference: 2.29)

New technology reports are generated in Phase H and drive the Change Management process. These should document new developments in potentially relevant technology. There is no recommended format for them.

15.2.30 Requirements Impact Statement

(Syllabus reference: 2.30)

This is an output of Phase H and is a response to a Request for Architecture Change. It documents an assessment of the changes and the recommendations for change to the architecture. The recommended contents are as follows:
- Reference to specific requirements
- Stakeholder priority of the requirements to date

- Phases to be revisited
- Phase to lead on requirements prioritization
- Results of phase investigations and revised priorities
- Recommendations on management of requirements
- Repository reference number

SEE ALSO
Chapter 14

15.3 Summary

This chapter has described key deliverables and processes from the ADM.

15.4 Test Yourself Questions

Q1: Which of the following is an advantage of using TOGAF over defining an architecture framework from scratch?

A. TOGAF contains a set of resources and methods for re-use.
B. TOGAF contains a Foundation Architecture.
C. TOGAF contains a breadth of tools.
D. TOGAF has a method which can be followed.
E. All of these

Q2: The Lead Architect in conjunction with … develops architecture principles:

A. The software development team
B. The sales team
C. The key business stakeholders
D. The finance team
E. The executive team

Q3: Which of the following best describes an understandable principle?

A. It is stable and enduring.
B. It captures a fundamental truth.
C. It is complete.
D. It is clear and unambiguous.
E. It is self-evident.

Q4:   Which of the following is not a business principle?
      A.   Primacy of Principles
      B.   Common Use Applications
      C.   Business Continuity
      D.   Compliance with the Law
      E.   Ease-of-use

Q5:   Which of the following is not built into the COBIT framework?
      A.   Maturity Models
      B.   Asset Management Model
      C.   Critical Success Factors
      D.   Key Goal Indicators
      E.   Key Performance Indicators

Q6:   Which of the following topics is not part of the suggested Request for
      Architecture Work document?
      A.   The sponsor organization name
      B.   The sponsor organization mission statement
      C.   A set of acceptance criteria
      D.   The time limits for the project
      E.   The description of resources available to the architecture project

Q7:   The Statement of Architecture Work is a response to the Request for
      Architecture Work. Which of the following describe it?
      A.   It contains a detailed description of the business functions in the
           organization.
      B.   It describes an overall plan to address the request for work
           including a schedule.
      C.   It is an output of Phase B: Business Architecture.
      D.   It lists the actors and their roles in the architecture work.
      E.   It includes a selection of the architecture model for the project.

Q8:   Which technique is used in Phase A: Architecture Vision to identify
      key stakeholders and their concerns?
      A.   Gap analysis
      B.   Requirements Impact Analysis
      C.   Business scenarios
      D.   All of these
      E.   Requirements change management

Q9: The Business Architecture generated in Phase B should describe all the following except:

A. A high-level description of the people and locations involved with key business functions

B. Impact Analysis report

C. Business Architecture Building Blocks

D. Candidate business Solution Building Blocks

E. Technical requirements for subsequent phases

Q10: When performing gap analysis during the Business Architecture phase, which of the following is not a valid response to the case of a Business Architecture Building Block from the Baseline Architecture found to be missing in the Target Architecture?

A. A review should occur.

B. If the building block was correctly eliminated, it should be added to the Target Architecture in the next iteration.

C. If the building block was correctly eliminated, it should be marked as such in an "Eliminated" cell.

D. If the building block was incorrectly eliminated, it should be reinstated to the architecture design in the next iteration.

E. If the building block was incorrectly eliminated, it should be recorded as an accidental omission.

Q11: The Technology Architecture generated in Phase D should describe all the following except:

A. A skills matrix and set of job descriptions

B. Gap analysis report

C. Requirements Traceability Analysis

D. Technology Architecture Models

E. Technical specification for each building block

Q12: Views and viewpoints are used by an architect to capture or model the design of a system architecture. Which of the following statements is true?

A. A view is the perspective of an individual stakeholder.

B. Different stakeholders always share the same views.

C. Some views do not have associated viewpoints.

D. A viewpoint is the perspective of an individual stakeholder.

E. Views and viewpoints are rarely used in TOGAF.

Q13: Which of the following statements describe generic building blocks?
   A. A building block is a package of functionality defined to meet the business needs.
   B. All of these
   C. A building block has published interfaces to access the functionality.
   D. A building block may be assembled from other building blocks.
   E. A building block may have multiple implementations.

Q14: Architecture Building Blocks are architecture documentation and models from the enterprise's:
   A. Solutions Continuum
   B. Architecture Vision
   C. Architecture Continuum
   D. Architecture Board
   E. CIO

Q15: Which of the following best describes the characteristics of Solution Building Blocks?
   A. They are defined in ADM Phase A and B.
   B. They define what products and components will implement the functionality.
   C. They are technology-aware.
   D. They fulfill business requirements.
   E. They capture business and technical requirements.

Q16: Which of the following are generated in the Impact Analysis in Phase E?
   A. A project list
   B. A time-oriented Migration Plan describing how existing systems will be migrated to the new architecture
   C. A set of measures of effectiveness for the projects
   D. A cost/benefit analysis for the proposed projects
   E. A cost estimate for the migration projects

Q17: The typical contents of an Architecture Design and Development Contract include:
   A. The scope of the architecture
   B. All of these

    C.   Architecture development and management processes and roles

    D.   Time window(s)

    E.   Architecture delivery and business metrics

Q18: Which of the following statements is not true?

    A.   Product Information is an input to Phase E.

    B.   When considering products, a document should be produced containing their functional descriptions.

    C.   When considering products, a document should be produced containing their architecture descriptions.

    D.   TOGAF does not provide a set of guidelines for reviewing Requests for Architecture Change.

    E.   The Business Users' Architecture Contract is used to manage changes to the enterprise architecture in Phase H.

Q19: Which of the following statements concerning New Technology Reports is true?

    A.   They are generated in Phase H.

    B.   They drive the Change Management process.

    C.   They should document new developments in potentially relevant technology.

    D.   There is no recommended format for them.

    E.   All of these

Q20: Which of the following are included in the recommended contents of a Requirements Impact Statement?

    A.   Stakeholders' priorities of the requirements to date

    B.   Phases to be revisited

    C.   Results of phase investigations and revised priorities

    D.   Recommendations on management of requirements

    E.   All of these

15.5 Recommended Reading

For this chapter the recommended sources of further information are included inline within each subsection rather than as a separate section here.

PART 3

TOGAF Foundation Architecture

Chapter 16

The Technical Reference Model (TRM)

16.1 Key Learning Points

This chapter describes the TOGAF Technical Reference Model (TRM), which is one part of the TOGAF Foundation Architecture, the other part being the Standards Information Base (SIB) that is described in the following chapter.

Key Points Explained

This chapter will help you to answer the following questions:

- What is the TOGAF Foundation Architecture?
- What is the purpose, structure, and use of the TRM?
- What is the Platform Services Taxonomy?
- What are the Application Platform Service Qualities?

> The TOGAF Foundation Architecture is a set of templates for creating the models needed to analyze the baseline and future state. The organization-specific architecture is created by populating the TOGAF Enterprise Continuum with Architecture Building Blocks that represent the components of the architecture and their embodiments as Solution Building Blocks.
> *Bill Estrem, "TOGAF to the Rescue"* (www.opengroup.org/downloads)

16.2 Introduction to the TOGAF Foundation Architecture

A Foundation Architecture is defined as follows:

"An architecture of building blocks and corresponding standards that supports all the Common Systems Architectures and, therefore, the complete computing environment."

The TOGAF Foundation Architecture is an architecture of generic services and functions that provides a foundation on which specific architectures and Architecture Building Blocks (ABBs) can be built. It comprises the Technical

Reference Model (TRM) and the Standards Information Base (SIB). Application of the TOGAF ADM to this Foundation Architecture is used to generate more specific enterprise architectures (see Section 16.3.1).

The major characteristics of the TOGAF Foundation Architecture are as follows:
- It reflects computing requirements and building blocks.
- It defines technology standards (open standards) for building blocks implementation.
- It provides direction for products and services.
- It reflects the function of a complete, robust computing environment used as a foundation.
- It reflects directions and strategies.

16.3 Purpose, Structure, and Use of the TRM
(Syllabus reference: 3.1.1)

16.3.1 Purpose
The purpose of the TRM is to facilitate definition of the standardized Application Platform and its associated interfaces. This is achieved by providing a widely-accepted core taxonomy, together with an appropriate visual representation of that taxonomy. Other entities are only addressed in the TRM insofar as they influence the Application Platform. The aim of this approach is to ensure that the higher-level building blocks that make up business solutions have a complete, robust platform on which to run.

16.3.2 Structure
The TRM has two main components:
1. A *taxonomy* that defines terminology, and provides a coherent description of the components and conceptual structure of an information system
2. A model, with an associated *TRM graphic*, that provides a visual representation of the taxonomy, as an aid to understanding

Figure 16-1 shows the high-level model of the TRM. The three main parts of the TRM (Application Software, Application Platform, and Communications Infrastructure) are connected by two interfaces (Application Platform Interface and Communications Infrastructure Interface).

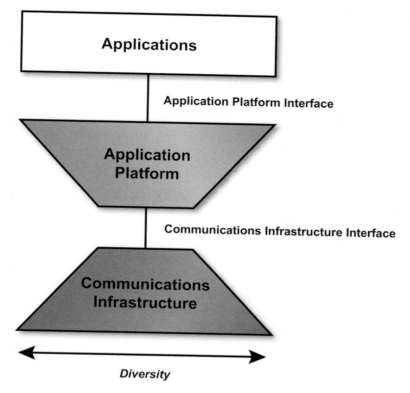

Figure 16.1: Technical Reference Model – High-Level Model View

Figure 16-1 emphasizes two major common architecture objectives:

1. **Application Portability**, via the Application Platform Interface, identifying the set of services that are to be made available in a standard way to applications via the platform
2. **Interoperability**, via the Communications Infrastructure Interface, identifying the set of Communications Infrastructure services that are to be built on in a standard way

Figure 16-2 shows the detail of the TRM. This highlights the platform service categories (see Section 16.4) together with the external environment entities, such as applications and Communications Infrastructure.

The following sections look at various elements from the TRM.

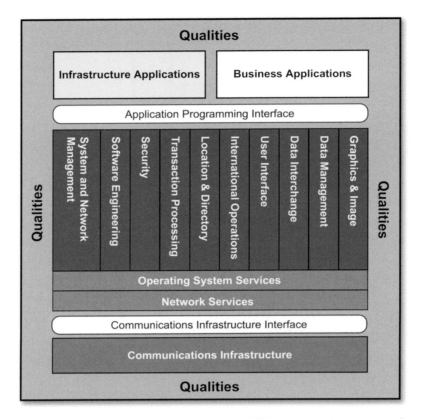

Figure 16.2: Detailed Technical Reference Model (Showing Service Categories)

16.3.2.1 Application Software

The TRM recognizes two categories of Application Software:

1. **Business Applications**, which implement business processes for an
    enterprise or vertical industry. These are specific to the enterprise or
    vertical industry. The internal structure of business applications relates
    closely to the specific Application Software configuration selected by
    an organization. Examples of business applications include patient
    record management services used in the medical industry; inventory
    management services used in the retail industry, geological data modeling
    services used in the petroleum industry, etc.

2. **Infrastructure Applications**, which provide general-purpose business
    functionality, based on infrastructure services. This is usually widespread
    commercial off-the-shelf (COTS) software, where it is uneconomic
    to consider custom implementation. Examples of applications in
    this category include electronic payment and funds transfer services,

electronic mail client services, calendaring and scheduling services, spreadsheet, presentation and document editing software, etc.

16.3.2.2 Application Platform Interface

The API specifies a complete interface between the Application Software and the underlying Application Platform across which all services are provided. A rigorous definition of the interface results in application portability, provided that both platform and application conform to it. For this to work, the API definition must include the syntax and semantics of not just the programmatic interface, but also all necessary protocol and data structure definitions.

16.3.2.3 Application Platform

The Application Platform is a single conceptual entity that includes Operating System Services, Network Services, and a generic set of platform services. This is the set of all possible services. A specific Target Architecture will contain only those services needed to support the required function. A typical architecture will also contain several Application Platforms; for example, a desktop client, file server, print server, internet server, database server, etc, each of which comprises a specific set of services to support the defined functionality.

16.3.2.4 Interfaces between Services

In addition to supporting Application Software through the Application Platform Interface (API), services in the Application Platform may support each other, either by openly specified interfaces or by private, unexposed interfaces. A key goal of architecture development is for service modules to be capable of replacement by other modules providing the same service functionality via the same service API.

16.3.2.5 Communications Infrastructure

The Communications Infrastructure provides the basic services to interconnect systems and provide the basic mechanisms for opaque transfer of data. It contains the hardware and software elements which make up the networking and physical communications links used by a system, and all the other systems connected to the network. It deals with the complex world of networks and the physical Communications Infrastructure, including switches, service providers, and the physical transmission media.

16.3.2.6 Communications Infrastructure Interface

The Communications Infrastructure Interface is the interface between the Application Platform and the Communications Infrastructure.

16.3.2.7 Qualities

Besides the set of components making up the TRM, there is also a set of attributes that are termed "qualities" that apply across all components. Examples of qualities, which typically must apply through all elements of an architecture, include manageability and security. Qualities are specified in detail during the development of a Target Architecture. Some qualities are easier than others to describe in terms of standards. For instance, support for a set of locales can be defined to be part of the specification for the international operation quality. Other qualities can better be specified in terms of measures rather than standards (e.g., performance).

16.3.3 Using the TRM

When building an architecture, users of TOGAF should assess their own requirements and select the services, interfaces, and standards that satisfy their own business needs. The objective of the TRM is to facilitate definition of the standardized Application Platform and its associated interfaces. Other entities are only addressed in the TRM insofar as they influence the Application Platform. The aim of this approach is to ensure that the higher-level building blocks which make up business solutions have a complete, robust platform on which to run.

It is important to recognize that the Application Platform in the TOGAF TRM is a single, generic, conceptual entity. From the viewpoint of the TOGAF TRM, the Application Platform contains all possible services. It is important to recognize that many of the real-world IT systems that are procured and used today come fully equipped with many advanced services. Service bundles are represented in a Technology Architecture in the form of building blocks. The IT architect must analyze the services actually needed in order to implement an IT infrastructure that meets the enterprise's business requirements in the optimal manner, and define the set of optimal Solution Building Blocks (SBBs) (real-world "platforms") to implement that architecture.

Other architecture models may be preferable for some enterprises. For example, an enterprise may prefer to represent the TOGAF taxonomy using a different form of graphic, which better captures legacy concepts and proves easier for internal communication purposes. Apart from the need to recognize that the structure embodied in the taxonomy is reflected in the structure of the SIB, there is no problem with using other architecture taxonomies and/or graphics with TOGAF. The core of TOGAF is its ADM: the TRM and the SIB are tools used in applying the ADM in the development of specific architectures. Provided consistency between the TRM and SIB are maintained, the TOGAF ADM is valid whatever the choice of specific taxonomy, TRM graphic, or SIB toolset.

16.4 Taxonomy of Application Platform Services
(Syllabus reference: 3.1.2)

The taxonomy of Platform Services provides a coherent description of an information system and is widely accepted as a useful, consistent structured definition of the Application Platform entity. It consists of a number of components termed "service categories", with further services defined within each category (see Table 16-1).

The taxonomy of the TOGAF TRM is used in structuring the TOGAF SIB, the database of industry standards endorsed by The Open Group.
A detailed description of the Service Categories and services within each is given in TOGAF 8.1.1, Enterprise Edition Part III: Enterprise Continuum, Detailed Platform Taxonomy.

Table 16.1: TRM Service Categories

Service Category	Description
Data Interchange Services	Data Interchange Services provide specialized support for the interchange of information between applications and the external environment. These services are designed to handle data interchange between applications on the same platform and applications on different (heterogeneous) platforms.
Data Management Services	Data Management Services provide for the management of data independently of the processes that create or use it, allow data to be maintained indefinitely, and shared among many processes.

Service Category	Description
Graphics and Imaging Services	Graphics and Imaging Services provide functions required for creating, storing, retrieving, and manipulating images.
International Operation Services	International Operation Services provide a set of services and interfaces that allow a user to define, select, and change between different culturally-related application environments supported by the particular implementation.
Location and Directory Services	Location and Directory Services provide specialized support for locating required resources and for mediation between service consumers and service providers.
Network Services	Network Services are provided to support distributed applications requiring data access and applications interoperability in heterogeneous or homogeneous networked environments.
Object-Oriented Provision of Services	This section shows how services are provided in an object-oriented manner. "Object Services" does not appear as a category in the TRM since all the individual object services are incorporated as appropriate in the other service categories.
Operating System Services	Operating System Services are responsible for the management of platform resources, including the processor, memory, files, and input and output. They generally shield applications from the implementation details of the machine.
Security Services	Security Services are necessary to protect sensitive information in the information system. The appropriate level of protection is determined based upon the value of the information to the business end users and the perception of threats to it.
Software Engineering Services	Software Engineering Services provide the tools for professional system developers appropriate to the development and maintenance of applications.
System and Network Management Services	System and Network Management Services provide for managing a wide variety of diverse resources of information systems.
Transaction Processing Services	Transaction Processing Services provide support for the online processing of information in discrete units called transactions, with assurance of the state of the information at the end of the transaction.
User Interface Services	User Interface Services define how users may interact with an application.

16.5 Taxonomy of Application Platform Service Qualities
(Syllabus reference 3.1.3)

A service quality describes behaviour such as adaptability or manageability.
Service qualities have a pervasive effect on the operation of most or all of the
functional service categories.

> **Qualities**
>
> During the process of architecture development, the architect must be aware of
> the qualities and the extent of their influence on the choice of software building
> blocks used in implementing the architecture. The best way of making sure that
> qualities are not forgotten is to create a quality matrix, describing the relationships
> between each functional service and the qualities that influence it.

The service qualities presently identified in the TRM taxonomy are:
- **Availability** (the degree to which something is available for use),
  including:
  — **Manageability**, the ability to gather information about the state of
    something and to control it
  — **Serviceability**, the ability to identify problems and take corrective
    action, such as to repair or upgrade a component in a running system
  — **Performance**, the ability of a component to perform its tasks in an
    appropriate time
  — **Reliability**, resistance to failure
  — **Recoverability**, the ability to restore a system to a working state after
    an interruption
  — **Locatability**, the ability of a system to be found when needed
- **Assurance**, including:
  — **Security**, the protection of information from unauthorized access
  — **Integrity**, the assurance that data has not been corrupted
  — **Credibility**, the level of trust in the integrity of the system and its data
- **Usability**, ease-of-operation by users, including:
  — **International Operation**, including multi-lingual and multi-cultural
    abilities
- **Adaptability**, including:
  — **Interoperability**, whether within or outside the organization (for

instance, interoperability of calendaring or scheduling functions may be key to the usefulness of a system)
— **Scalability**, the ability of a component to grow or shrink its performance or capacity appropriately to the demands of the environment in which it operates
— **Portability**, of data, people, applications, and components
— **Extensibility**, the ability to accept new functionality
— The ability to offer access to services in new paradigms such as object-orientation, or web-services

16.6 Summary

The TOGAF Technical Reference Model (TRM) provides a model and core taxonomy of generic platform services. It can be used to build any system architecture. A taxonomy defines terminology and provides a coherent description of the components and conceptual structure of an information system. The taxonomy of platform services defines terminology and provides a coherent description of an information system. It is a widely accepted, useful, consistent structural definition of the Application Platform entity, although it should be noted that it is not intended to be an exclusive or an optimal definition. The taxonomy of Application Platform Service Qualities provides a number of "qualities", also termed non-functional requirements, attributes or "ilities", which an architect must be aware of when implementing the architecture. The TOGAF ADM is not dependent on the TRM and can successfully be used without reference to it. The TRM is used to structure the TOGAF Standards Information Base.

16.7 Test Yourself Questions

Q1:   Which of the following is not a characteristic of the TOGAF Foundation Architecture?
   A.   It reflects general building blocks.
   B.   It defines open standards for building blocks implementation.
   C.   It provides open systems standards.
   D.   It provides guidelines for testing collections of systems.
   E.   It reflects general computing requirements.

Q2:   Which of the following best describes the purpose of the TRM?
   A.   To provide a framework for IT governance
   B.   To provide a visual model, terminology, and coherent description
        of components and structure of an information system
   C.   To provide a list of standards
   D.   To provide a method for architecture development
   E.   To provide a system engineering viewpoint on a possible solution

Q3:   Which of the following statements about the Taxonomy of Platform
      Services is true?
   A.   It provides a description of a specific vertical industry
        information system.
   B.   It defines a number of service qualities.
   C.   It provides a widely accepted, useful definition of an Application
        Platform entity.
   D.   It is used in structuring the III-RM.
   E.   It provides a list of standards.

Q4:   Which of the following is not a service category in the TRM?
   A.   Software Engineering Services
   B.   Security Services
   C.   Operating System Services
   D.   Object Services
   E.   User Interface Services

Q5:   Which of the following is a service within the Location and Directory
      Service Category defined in the TRM?
   A.   Electronic mail services
   B.   Service location services
   C.   Run-time environment services
   D.   Non-repudiation services
   E.   Database services

Q6:   Which of the following is not a quality defined in the Taxonomy of Service Qualities for Availability?

A.   Manageability: The ability to gather information about the state of something and to control it.

B.   Recoverability: The ability to restore a system after an interruption.

C.   Serviceability: The ability to repair or upgrade a component in a running system.

D.   Reliability: The resistance to failure.

E.   Scalability: The ability of a component to grow or shrink its performance or capacity appropriately.

16.8 Recommended Reading

The following are recommended sources of further information for this chapter:

- TOGAF 8.1.1 Enterprise Edition Part III: Enterprise Continuum, Introduction to the Enterprise Continuum
- TOGAF 8.1.1 Enterprise Edition Part III: Enterprise Continuum, The Enterprise Continuum in Detail
- TOGAF 8.1.1 Enterprise Edition Part III: Enterprise Continuum, Foundation Architecture – Technical Reference Model
- TOGAF 8.1.1 Enterprise Edition Part III: Enterprise Continuum, Detailed Platform Taxonomy

Chapter 17

Standards Information Base (SIB)

17.1 Key Learning Points

This chapter describes the Standards Information Base (SIB).

Key Points Explained

This chapter will help you to answer the following questions:
- What is the Standards Information Base (SIB)?
- How to access the SIB?
- How to use the SIB?
- How can the SIB be used to check for global standards?

17.2 Introduction to the SIB

The SIB is a database of facts and guidance about information systems standards. The standards included are drawn from a number of sources including:
- International Standards Organization (ISO)
- Institute of Electrical and Electronic Engineers (IEEE)
- World Wide Web Consortium (W3C)
- Object Management Group (OMG)
- Internet Society
- The Open Group

The SIB has three main uses, as shown in Table 17-1.

Table 17.1: Uses of the SIB

Use	Description
Architecture Development	The SIB is a resource for organizations creating an architecture for their information systems. It contains information about the standards that may be used to populate an architecture. The SIB can be used to dynamically generate lists, structured according to the TOGAF TRM taxonomy, of the standards endorsed by The Open Group for use in open systems architectures.
Acquisition/Procurement	An organization planning a procurement can use the SIB to ensure that the procurement gives a clear statement of technical requirements.
General Information	The SIB is also a source of information about relevant IT standards.

17.3 Access to the SIB
(Syllabus reference: 3.2.1)

The SIB is held in a web-accessible database. The SIB home page shown in Figure 17-1 is the usual starting point. From the SIB home page, there are a number of options:
- Search the SIB according to your own defined criteria
- View the complete SIB
- Learn more about the SIB

17.4 Searching the SIB
(Syllabus reference 3.2.2)

17.4.1 Getting Started
First, go to the Standards Information Base home page (www.opengroup. org/sib) as shown in Figure 17-1.

The home page provides four hyperlinks:
- Search it – generates a form to guide the search for specific standards or sets of standards.
- View it – generates a full summary listing of the entire SIB, structured according to the TOGAF Technical Reference Model taxonomy.

Figure 17.1: SIB Home Page (www.opengroup.org/sib)

- Help – links to an explanatory page giving information on the structure of an entry in the SIB.
- Learn more about it – links to a page of information giving an overview of the SIB.

The following examples are intended to provide an initial guide through the different resources available, and to provide readers with an understanding of the wide range of information available, starting from the SIB home page. Further examples are provided in the TOGAF document itself and are recommended reading.

The standards included in the SIB have all been adopted as Open Group standards. This means the standards have been endorsed by The Open Group as fit-for-purpose in architecture specification and procurement.

Example 1: Viewing the Entire SIB

From the SIB home page, click the "View it" hyperlink.

The result is a full summary listing of the SIB (shown in Figure 17-2 and Figure 17-3), represented as a series of tables, one for each of the major service categories in the TOGAF Technical Reference Model taxonomy. The hyperlinks at the head of the page provide links to the start of each service category table.

Figure 17.2: SIB "View it" Page with Service Categories Listed

If you select a particular Service Category, a table of standards is then listed; for example, as in Figure 17-3.

Selecting the Details link will then show specific information as shown in Figure 17-4.

The SIB entry contains information about a standard and also a hyperlink to the web for the responsible standards organization.

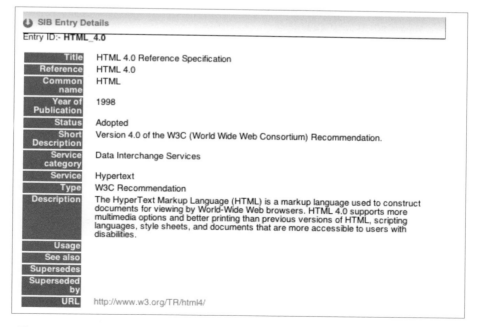

🔘 Reference	🔘 Year	🔘 Title	🔘 Summary	🔘 SIB Status
ISBN: 0-201-62628-4	1993	Portable Document Format Reference Manual	The Official Guide to the Portable Document Format (PDF). (Details)	Adopted
HTML 3.2	1997	HTML 3.2 Reference Specification	Version 3.2 of the W3C (World Wide Web Consortium) Recommendation. (Details)	Adopted
HTML 4.0	1998	HTML 4.0 Reference Specification	Version 4.0 of the W3C (World Wide Web Consortium) Recommendation. (Details)	Adopted
ISO/IEC 10918	1994/1995	Information technology -- Digital compression and coding of continuous-tone still images	A multi-part International Standard that collectively defines JPEG. (Details)	Adopted
Comprises the following parts:				
	1995	ISO/IEC 10918-2:1995 Information technology -- Digital compression and coding of continuous-tone still images: Compliance testing	Compliance testing for compression and coding of continuous-tone still images.	
	1995	ISO/IEC DIS 10918-3 Information technology -- Digital compression and coding of continuous-tone still images: Extensions	Extensions to Standards for digital compression and coding of continuous-tone still images.	

Figure 17.3: Standards Listing for the Data Interchange Service Category (partial list)

Figure 17.4: Example SIB Entry

17.4.2   Anatomy of a SIB Entry

An individual SIB entry is composed as shown in Table 17-2.

Table 17.2: Anatomy of a SIB Entry

SIB Field	Description
Title	This is the title of the standard.
Reference	The formal reference to the Standard. For IETF RFCs this is IETF RFC nnnn; for an International Standard it is of the form ISO/IEC nnnn.
Common Name	If the standard has a colloquial name which it is well known by as well as its formal title, then that is given here; e.g., JPEG, XBD Issue 6.
Year of Publication	The year of official publication of the standard.
Status	One of *Adopted, Pending, Withdrawn, Superseded,* or *Obsolete.*
Short Description	A brief description of what the standard is about. Used in the results page after a search, in place of the Description field, and in the View Full SIB (100 characters max).
Service Category	As defined by the TOGAF TRM; e.g., Data Interchange Services, Operating System Services, etc.
Service	A specific service within a Service Category; for example, Hypertext within the Data Interchange Services Service Category.
Type	One of: • The Open Group Product Standard, Technical Standard, or Guide • IEEE Standard • IETF RFC • Internet Standard • International Standard • ITU Standard • W3C Recommendation • Other
Description	A full description of what the standard is about, shown when "Full details" is displayed. Unlimited length.
Usage	Notes on using this standard.
See Also	Used for cross-references.
Supersedes	If this standard supersedes another.
Superseded by	If this standard is superseded by another.
URL	Link to more information.

Example 2: Searching for Standards

The Search link available from the SIB home page allows a set of criteria to be input and entries that match returned. The search form is shown in Figure 17-5.

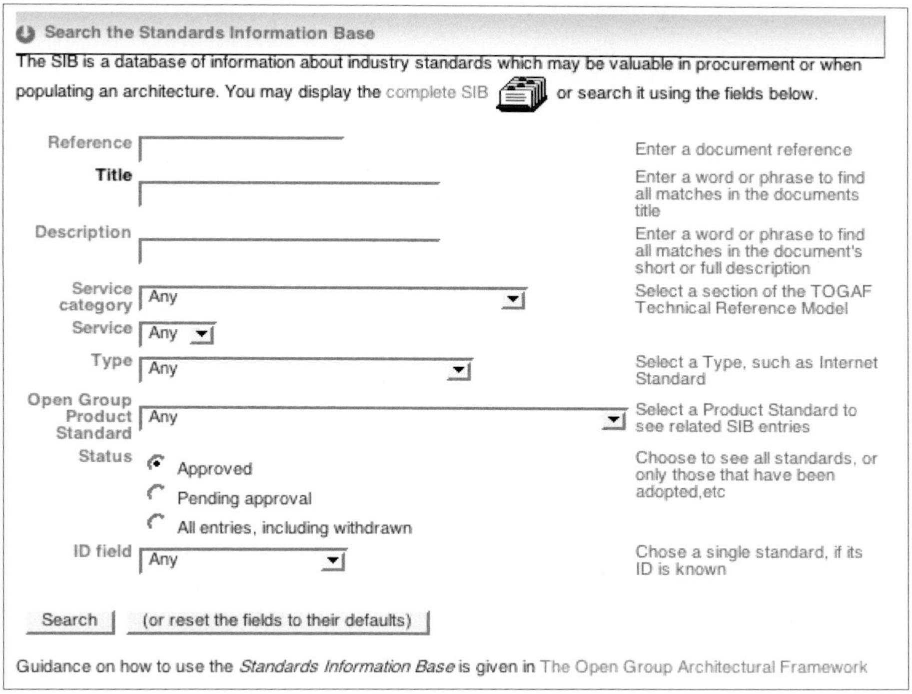

Figure 17.5: SIB Search Screen

The Service Category drop-down box contains a list of Service categories from the TOGAF TRM. When you select a Services category (without clicking the Search button), then when you select the Service drop-down menu a list of individual services within the Service Category will appear.

For example, if you select the Data Interchange Services Category, and then pull down the Hypertext service, followed by the Search button, a set of search results for all standards in the SIB related to hypertext service is returned.

Table 17-3 shows the meaning of various values of the Status field.

Table 17.3: SIB Status Values

Value	Description
Adopted	The item has been formally adopted by The Open Group for use in TOGAF and for use in Product Standards.
Pending	The item is awaiting formal adoption into the SIB – it fits the requirements for adoption. These items will often be a new Open Group Technical Standard or a standard referenced in the specification.
Obsolete	The item has been superseded by another more recent specification or standard in the SIB. It is retained as an historical record and to preserve references to Product Standards and thus to products with the Open Brand certification mark.
Other	The item falls outside of the above definitions. This category covers items under consideration; items that are referenced in an Open Group Preliminary Specification or Guide; and other relevant items, including specifications and standards developed by consortia and other bodies which work closely with The Open Group. Items in this category are *not* regarded as being in the SIB.

17.5 Using the Information in the SIB
(Syllabus reference 3.2.3)

The SIB provides the architect with a gateway to a uniquely powerful set of tools for defining the standards that an architecture is to mandate, and, in the cases where associated certification programs are in place, for checking the availability in the marketplace of products guaranteed to conform to those standards.

The lists of standards returned are structured according to the TRM taxonomy of Platform Services and can be used in open systems architectures.

Example 3 – Searching the SIB for Available Products
In this example, a search is made to locate available certified products for The Open Group's UNIX® Product Standards.

In the search screen shown in Figure 17-6, the Services Category Operating System Services is selected, UNIX is entered in the Title and Description

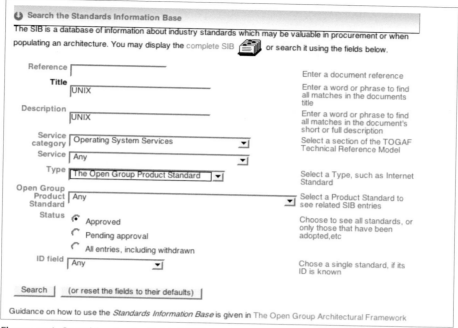

Figure 17.6: Searching for Available UNIX Products

fields to narrow the search, and the document type selected is The Open Group Product Standard. An Open Group Product Standard is an integrated set of standards together with an associated certification program. For the UNIX system, the certification program is known as The Open Brand[1]. Selecting the search button, the matches are then returned as shown in Figure 17-7.

If the Details link is then selected, a page of information is displayed. Selecting the URL link at the foot of that page will then take you to The Open Group's Open Brand online database where a page of further information and links is provided. This provides overview information on the Product Standard as shown in Figure 17-8.

The information on the Product Standard also contains links to information especially relevant to procurement; for example, conformance statements containing information on implementation options, test suites, and a list of Registered Products as shown in Figure 17-9.

---

1 For information on The Open Brand certification program, see www.opengroup.org/openbrand.

The search criteria were :-

Title	matches	UNIX
Description	matches	UNIX
Service category	is	Operating System Services
Type	is	The Open Group Product Standard
Status	is	Approved

4 entries selected.

Service category and Type	Reference and status	Title and Year	Short Description	Other views
Operating System Services The Open Group Product Standard	X03XY (UNIX 03) Adopted	UNIX 03 2003	The foundation product standard for systems conforming to Version 3 of the Single UNIX Specification	Details Full SIB Comment
Operating System Services The Open Group Product Standard	X/Open XW Adopted	UNIX 98 Workstation 1998	The UNIX 98 Workstation Product Standard.	Details Full SIB Comment
Operating System Services The Open Group Product Standard	X/Open XX Adopted	UNIX 98 1998	The UNIX 98 Product Standard.	Details Full SIB Comment
Operating System Services The Open Group Product Standard	X/Open XU Adopted	UNIX 95 1995	Defines a consolidated platform for the support of a wide range of applications.	Details Full SIB Comment

Figure 17.7: SIB Search Results for UNIX Product Standards

UNIX 03

Category: Operating System and Languages [XY]

The UNIX 03 Product Standard is the mark for systems conforming to Version 3 of the Single UNIX Specification. It is a significantly enhanced version of the UNIX 98 Product Standard. The mandatory enhancements include alignment with ISO/IEC 9989:1999 C Programming Language, IEEE Std 1003.1-2001 and ISO/IEC 9945:2002. This Product Standard includes the following mandatory Product Standards: Internationalized System Calls and Libraries Extended V3,Commands and Utilities V4, C Language V2, and Internationalized Terminal Interfaces.

Product Standards are explained in Practical Guide to the Open Brand

Click for a Web version of the Product Standard

Click for full text of the Product Standard Definition: in PDF Format

Figure 17.8: Part 1 of the UNIX 03 Product Standard Page

For a detailed explanation of how the standards generated in this way are used, refer to TOGAF 8.1.1 Enterprise Edition Part II: Architecture Development Method (ADM), which describes how to use the complete TOGAF Foundation Architecture as a basis for defining (by service) all the

Conformance Statement Questionnaires:

CSQ for UNIX 03 Product Standard

CSQ for Internationalized System Calls & Libraries Extd V3 Product Standard

CSQ for Commands and Utilities V4 Product Standard

CSQ for C Language V2 Product Standard

CSQ for Internationalized Terminal Interfaces Product Standard

Test Suites:

VSX5 , and VSX4 , and VSU5 , and VSTH , and VSART , (and optionally VSRT, VSRTE, VSTRC) , and VSC5 , and (Plum Hall , or Perennial CVSA)

Present in UNIX 03 Product Standard(s)

Go to Registered Products

Figure 17.9: Part 2 of the UNIX 03 Product Standard Page

standards that make up the Target Technology Architecture, and all the Solution Building Blocks (SBBs) that will be used to implement it.

17.6 Summary

The Standards Information Base is a public web-accessible database of standards adopted by The Open Group. It is intended to represent the definitive list of The Open Group standards, and be a valuable resource to third parties, who are able to use it as a stable reference point for procurement. The set of standards has been developed within The Open Group and by other standards bodies, and is structured according to the TOGAF Technical Reference Model (TRM). The URL for accessing the SIB is www.opengroup.org/sib.

17.7 Test Yourself Questions

Q1:   Which of the following is a standards organization whose standards are not currently listed in the SIB?

A.   Institute of Electrical Engineers

B.   The Open Group

C.   International Standards Organization

D.   Object Management Group

E.   Internet Society

Q2:   Which of the following is not a use of the SIB?
A.   To identify and provide a taxonomy of platform services
B.   To identify and provide standards information for procurement
C.   To guide procurers on applicable standards
D.   To identify and provide a reference on standards information to populate architectures
E.   To identify and provide IT standards information

Q3:   Which of the following is not a service category in the SIB?
A.   Software Engineering Services
B.   Security Services
C.   Operating System Services
D.   Object Services
E.   Network Services

Q4:   To search for available products for an Open Group certification program, which is the most applicable search field to narrow down the search?
A.   Reference
B.   Title
C.   Service category
D.   Type
E.   Open Group Product Standard

Q5:   Which of the following status values indicates that a standard is a current formal standard of The Open Group?
A.   Other
B.   Pending
C.   Preliminary
D.   Obsolete
E.   Adopted

Q6:   In which phase of the ADM is the SIB used as an input?
A.   Phase A
B.   Phase B
C.   Phase C
D.   Phase D
E.   Phase E

17.8 Recommended Reading

The following are recommended sources of further information for this chapter:

- TOGAF 8.1.1 Enterprise Edition Part III: Enterprise Continuum, Introduction to the Enterprise Continuum
- TOGAF 8.1.1 Enterprise Edition Part III: Enterprise Continuum, Detailed Platform Taxonomy
- TOGAF 8.1.1 Enterprise Edition Part III: Enterprise Continuum, Foundation Architecture – Standards Information Base
- The Open Group Standards Information Base: www.opengroup.org/sib
- The Open Group Certification Programs: www.opengroup.org/certification

PART 4

The Enterprise Continuum

Chapter 18

Introduction to the Enterprise Continuum

18.1 Key Learning Points

This chapter provides an introduction to the Enterprise Continuum.

This chapter will help you answer the following questions:

- What is the Enterprise Continuum?
- How is the Enterprise Continuum used in developing an architecture?

18.2 Overview of the Enterprise Continuum

(Syllabus reference: 4.)

The "Enterprise Continuum" is a phrase that denotes the combination of two complementary concepts: the Architecture Continuum and the Solutions Continuum (which are discussed in detail in the following two chapters). This chapter of the Study Guide looks in detail at the high-level concept of the Enterprise Continuum.

Any architecture is context-specific; for example, there are architectures that are specific to individual customers, industries, subsystems, products, and services. Architects, on both the buy-side and supply-side, must have at their disposal a consistent language to effectively communicate the differences between architectures. Such a language will enable engineering efficiency and the effective use of commercial-off-the-shelf (COTS) product functionality. The Enterprise Continuum provides that consistent language. Not only does the Enterprise Continuum represent an aid to communication, it also represents an aid to organizing re-usable architecture and solution assets (in the virtual repository). As an organization proceeds through the development of an architecture it can reach into the virtual repository to re-use an existing asset, or add a newly developed asset to the repository for later re-use.

18.2.1 The Enterprise Continuum and Architecture Re-Use

The "virtual repository" that is the Enterprise Continuum consists of all the architecture assets; that is, models, patterns, architecture descriptions, and other artifacts produced during application of the ADM. These can exist both within the enterprise and in the IT industry at large, and are considered the set of assets available for the development of architectures for the enterprise. Examples of assets "within the enterprise" are the deliverables of previous architecture work, which are available for re-use. Examples of assets "in the IT industry at large" are the wide variety of industry reference models and architecture patterns that exist, and are continually emerging, including those that are highly generic (such as TOGAF's own Technical Reference Model (TRM)); those specific to certain aspects of IT (such as a web services architecture); those specific to certain types of information processing (such as e-Commerce); and those specific to certain vertical industries (such as the ARTS data model from the retail industry). The decision as to which architecture assets a specific enterprise considers part of its own Enterprise Continuum will normally form part of the overall architecture governance function within the enterprise concerned.

18.2.2 Using the Enterprise Continuum within the ADM

The TOGAF Architecture Development Method (ADM) describes the process of moving from the TOGAF Foundation Architecture to an enterprise-specific architecture (or set of architectures). This process makes use of the elements of the TOGAF Foundation Architecture and other relevant architecture assets, components, and building blocks. At relevant places throughout the TOGAF ADM, there are reminders to consider which architecture assets from the Enterprise Continuum the architect should use. TOGAF itself provides two reference models for consideration for inclusion in an organization's Enterprise Continuum: the TOGAF Foundation Architecture and the Integrated Information Infrastructure Reference Model (III-RM).

18.3 Summary

The Enterprise Continuum is a virtual repository for architecture assets. It enables the organization of re-usable architecture and solution assets. It is also an aid to communication between all architects involved in building and procuring an architecture by providing a common language and terminology. This, in turn, enables efficiency in engineering and effective use of COTS products.

18.4 Test Yourself Questions

Q1:   Which of the following statements does not apply to the Enterprise Continuum?

A.   It is a virtual repository of all known architecture assets and artifacts in the IT industry.

B.   It is a virtual repository of all architecture assets and artifacts which the enterprise is considering in its own architecture project.

C.   It provides a taxonomy for classifying architecture assets.

D.   It is an important aid to communication for architects on both the buy and supply-side.

E.   It is an aid to organization of re-usable and solution assets.

Q2:   Which of the following in the Enterprise Continuum is an example of "assets within the enterprise"?

A.   Deliverables from previous architecture work

B.   Industry reference models and patterns

C.   The TOGAF TRM

D.   The Zachman Framework

E.   The ARTS data model

Q3:   Which of the following in the Enterprise Continuum is not an example of "assets within the IT industry at large"?

A.   The TOGAF TRM

B.   The Zachman Framework

C.   IT-specific models, such as web services

D.   The ARTS data model

E.   Deliverables from previous architecture work

Q4:   Which of the following answers complete the next phrase? The criteria for including source materials in an organization specific Enterprise Continuum …

A.   Is decided in Phase A of the ADM

B.   Is part of the IT governance process

C.   Is decided by the choices made in the Foundation Architecture

D.   Is decided by the stakeholders

E.   Is decided by the CEO

Q5:   Which of the following complete the sentence? The Enterprise
       Continuum aids communication …
       A.   Within enterprises
       B.   Between enterprises
       C.   With vendor organizations
       D.   By providing a consistent language to communicate the
            differences between architectures
       E.   All of these

18.5 Recommended Reading

The following are recommended sources of further information for this
chapter:

- TOGAF 8.1.1 Enterprise Edition Part III: Enterprise Continuum,
  Introduction to the Enterprise Continuum

Chapter 19

The Architecture Continuum

19.1 Key Learning Points

This chapter describes the Architecture Continuum, which is a part of the Enterprise Continuum.

Key Points Explained

This chapter will help you to answer the following questions:
- What is the Architecture Continuum?
- How is the Architecture Continuum used in developing an architecture?
- What is the relationship of the Architecture Continuum to the Solutions Continuum?

Definition of "Continuum"

Noun: a continuous extent of something, no part of which is different from any other

Source: Wiktionary.org

19.2 The Concept of the Architecture Continuum

(Syllabus reference: 4.1.1)

There is a continuum of architectures, Architecture Building Blocks (ABBs), and architecture models that are relevant to the task of constructing an enterprise-specific architecture, that are termed by TOGAF as the Architecture Continuum. These are shown in Figure 19-1.

Together with the Solutions Continuum (see Chapter 20), the Architecture Continuum forms the Enterprise Continuum, a "virtual repository" of all the architecture assets.

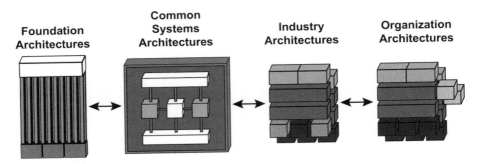

Figure 19.1: The Architecture Continuum

19.3 Moving Around the Architecture Continuum
(Syllabus reference: 4.1.2)

Figure 19-1 illustrates how architectures are developed, drawing on existing architectures. The arrows in the diagram illustrate the bi-directional flows between different architectures. The leftward arrows focus on meeting enterprise and business needs, whilst the rightwards arrows focus on leveraging architecture building components and building blocks.

The enterprise needs and business requirements are addressed in increasing detail from left to right. The architect will typically look to find re-usable architecture elements toward the left of the continuum. When elements are not found, the requirements for the missing elements are passed to the left of the continuum for incorporation.

19.4 The Continuum as a Repository of Re-Usable Architecture Building Blocks
(Syllabus reference: 4.1.3)

Within the Architecture Continuum there are a number of re-usable Architecture Building Blocks – the models of architectures. This can be thought of as a "framework-within-a-framework" for developing architectures. An architect should look to re-use as much as possible from the continuum as is relevant to the project scope. The Architecture Building Blocks are discussed in more detail in the following sections.

19.4.1 Foundation Architecture

A Foundation Architecture is an architecture of building blocks and corresponding standards that supports all the Common Systems Architectures and, therefore, the complete computing environment. This is covered in more detail in Chapter 16.

19.4.2 Common Systems Architectures

Common Systems Architectures guide the selection and integration of specific services from the Foundation Architecture to create an architecture useful for building common solutions across a wide number of relevant domains. Examples of Common Systems Architectures include: Security Architecture, Management Architecture, Network Architecture, etc.

The TOGAF Integrated Information Infrastructure Reference Model (III-RM; see TOGAF 8.1.1 Enterprise Edition Part III: Enterprise Continuum, Integrated Information Infrastructure Reference Model) is a Common Systems Architecture that focuses on the requirements, building blocks, and standards relating to the vision of Boundaryless Information Flow.

19.4.3 Industry Architectures

Industry Architectures guide the integration of common systems components with industry-specific components, and guide the creation of industry solutions for specific customer problems within a particular industry.

A typical example of an industry-specific component is a data model representing the business functions and processes specific to a particular vertical industry, such as the Retail industry's "Active Store" architecture, or an Industry Architecture that incorporates the Petrotechnical Open Software Corporation (POSC) (www.posc.orw) data model.

19.4.4 Enterprise Architectures

Enterprise architectures are the most relevant to the IT customer community, since they describe and guide the final deployment of user-written or third-party components that constitute effective solutions for particular enterprises.

IEEE Std 1003.23-1998, Guide for Developing User Organization Open System Environment (OSE) Profiles, provides a method for identifying and documenting an organization's operational requirements, the IT and IS services needed to support those requirements, and the standards, standards options, interim solutions, and products that will provide the needed services.

There may be a continuum of enterprise architectures that are needed to effectively cover the organization's requirements by defining the enterprise architecture in increasing levels of detail. Alternatively, this might result in several more detailed enterprise architectures for specific entities within the global enterprise.

19.5 The Relationship to the Solutions Continuum
(Syllabus reference: 4.1.4)

(The Solutions Continuum is described in Chapter 20.)

The relationship between the Architecture Continuum and the Solutions Continuum is one of guidance, direction, and support. The Enterprise Continuum should not be interpreted as representing strictly chained relationships. Enterprise architectures could have components from a Common Systems Architecture, and enterprise solutions could contain a product or service. The relationships depicted in Figure 19-2 are a best case for the ideal use of architecture and solution components.

The beginning and the end of the Enterprise Continuum lie in a Foundation Architecture, which serves as a repository of re-usable guidelines and standards. For The Open Group, this Foundation Architecture is the Technical Reference Model (TRM) and Standards Information Base (SIB).

> Your architecture organization will have to deal with each type of architecture described above. For example, it is recommended that you have your own Foundation Architecture that governs all of your IT systems. You should also have your own Common Systems Architectures that govern major shared infrastructure systems. You may have your own industry-specific architectures that govern the way your IT systems must behave within your industry. Finally, any given department within your business may need its own individual enterprise architecture to govern the IT systems within that department.

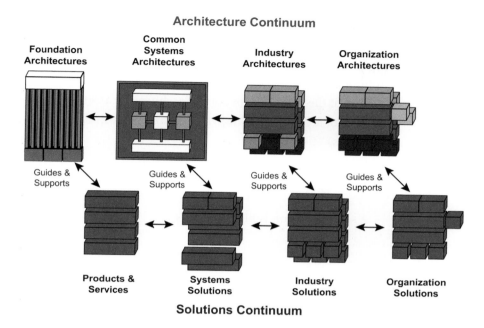

Figure 19.2: The Enterprise Continuum

19.6 Summary

The Architecture Continuum is part of an organization's Enterprise
Continuum and is supported by the Solutions Continuum (see Chapter
20). It offers a consistent way to define and understand the generic rules,
representations, and relationships in an information system, and it represents
a conceptual structuring of re-usable architecture assets.

The Architecture Continuum shows the relationships among foundational
frameworks (such as the TOGAF Foundation Architecture), Common
Systems Architectures (such as the III-RM), industry architectures, and
enterprise architectures. It is also a useful tool to discover commonality and
eliminate unnecessary redundancy.

19.7 Test Yourself Questions

Q1:   Which of the following responses does not complete the next
      sentence? The continuum of architectures within the Architecture
      Continuum are:
      A.   Part of the virtual repository of architecture assets
      B.   A set of architectures known as Architecture Building Blocks
           (ABBs)
      C.   Part of the set of architecture assets within the Enterprise
           Continuum
      D.   A set of models used to construct enterprise-specific architectures
      E.   A set of Solution Building Blocks

Q2:   The following different types of architectures are usually shown when
      illustrating the Architecture Continuum, except:
      A.   Organization Architectures
      B.   Gothic Architectures
      C.   Foundation Architectures
      D.   Industry Architectures
      E.   Common Systems Architectures

Q3:   Which of the following responses does not complete the next
      sentence? When moving around the Architecture Continuum, …
      A.   The architect looks towards the left of the continuum for re-usable
           architecture elements.
      B.   As you move right there is a progression from Horizontal (IT-
           focused) to Vertical (business-focused).
      C.   Enterprise-specific needs and requirements are addressed in more
           detail as you move to the right.
      D.   As you move right there is a progression from a generalization to
           specialization.
      E.   When elements are not found, the requirements must be passed to
           the right for incorporation.

Q4:   Which of the following statements are true? The TOGAF Integrated
      Information Infrastructure Reference Model (III-RM):
      A.   Is an example of a Common Systems Architecture
      B.   Is an example of an Industry Architecture
      C.   Is an example of an Enterprise Architecture

D.   Is part of the TOGAF Foundation Architecture

E.   Is required for use in the ADM

Q5:   Complete the following sentence. It is recommended that you have your own Foundation Architecture:

A.   That governs the way your IT systems must behave in your industry

B.   That governs all of your IT systems

C.   That governs all of the IT systems within a specific department

D.   That governs major shared infrastructure systems

E.   All of these

19.8 Recommended Reading

The following are recommended sources of further information for this chapter:

- TOGAF 8.1.1 Enterprise Edition Part III: Enterprise Continuum, Introduction to the Enterprise Continuum
- TOGAF 8.1.1 Enterprise Edition Part III: Enterprise Continuum, The Enterprise Continuum in Detail

Chapter 20

The Solutions Continuum

20.1 Key Learning Points

This chapter describes the Solutions Continuum, which is part of the Enterprise Continuum.

Key Points Explained

This chapter will help you to answer the following questions:

- What is the Solutions Continuum?
- How is the Solutions Continuum used to develop an architecture?

20.2 The Concept of the Solutions Continuum

(Syllabus reference: 4.2.1)

The Solutions Continuum, shown in Figure 20-1, represents the implementations of the architectures at the corresponding levels of the Architecture Continuum. At each level in the Solutions Continuum there is a set of reference building blocks that represent a solution to the business requirements at that level. A populated Solutions Continuum can be regarded as a re-use library.

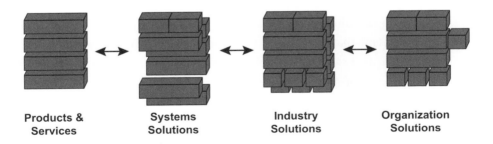

Figure 20.1: The Solutions Continuum

20.3 Moving Around the Solutions Continuum
(Syllabus reference: 4.2.2)

In Figure 20-1 the left-to-right direction focuses on providing solutions value; that is, products and services provide value in creating systems solutions. Systems solutions value is used to create industry solutions, and industry solutions are used to create enterprise solutions (also termed customer solutions). The right-to-left direction focuses on addressing enterprise needs.

The solution types within the Solutions Continuum are looked at in detail in the following sections.

20.3.1 Products and Services
Products are separately procurable hardware, software, or service entities. Products are the fundamental providers of capabilities.

20.3.2 Systems Solutions
A "systems solution" is an implementation of a Common Systems Architecture comprising a set of products and services. Systems solutions represent collections of common requirements and capabilities, rather than those specific to a particular customer or industry. Examples of systems solutions include an enterprise management system product or a security system product.

20.3.3 Industry Solutions
An "industry solution" is an implementation of an Industry Architecture, which provides re-usable packages of common components and services specific to an industry. Industry solutions are industry-specific, aggregate procurements that are ready to be tailored to an individual organization's requirements. Examples include a physical database schema or an industry-specific point-of-service device.

20.3.4 Enterprise Solutions
An "enterprise solution" is an implementation of the enterprise architecture that provides the required business functions. Because solutions are designed for specific business operations, they contain the highest amount of unique content in order to accommodate the people and processes of specific organizations.

20.4 The Solutions Continuum as a Repository of Re-Usable Solution Building Blocks

(Syllabus reference: 4.2.3)

A populated Solutions Continuum can be regarded as a solutions inventory or re-use library, which can add significant value to the task of managing and implementing improvements to the IT environment.

20.5 Summary

The Solutions Continuum is part of an organization's Enterprise Continuum. It represents implementations of the architectures at the corresponding levels of the Architecture Continuum. At each level, the Solutions Continuum is a population of the architecture with reference building blocks – either purchased products or built components – that represent a solution to the enterprise's business needs. A populated Solutions Continuum can be considered as a solutions inventory or re-use library, which can add significant value to the task of managing and implementing improvements to the IT environment.

20.6 Test Yourself Questions

Q1: Which of the following responses does not complete the next sentence? The Solutions Continuum is:

A. A set of reference building blocks

B. A set of reference building blocks known as Architecture Building Blocks (ABBs)

C. Part of the set of architecture assets within the Enterprise Continuum

D. A representation of the architectures at the corresponding level in the Architecture Continuum

E. A set of Solution Building Blocks

Q2: The following reference building blocks are usually shown when illustrating the Solutions Continuum, except:

A. Systems libraries

B. Organization solutions

C. Products and services

      D.   Systems solutions

      E.   Industry solutions

Q3:   Which of the following statements is not true?

      A.   Products are separately procurable hardware, software, or service entities.

      B.   A "systems solution" is an implementation of a Common Systems Architecture comprising a set of products and services.

      C.   An "industry solution" is an implementation of an Industry Architecture.

      D.   An example of an industry solution is a physical database schema.

      E.   An example of a systems solution is an industry-specific point-of-service device.

Q4:   Which of the following statements is not true?

      A.   Products are the fundamental providers of capabilities.

      B.   Systems solutions represent collections of common requirements and capabilities.

      C.   Industry solutions are industry-specific, aggregate procurements.

      D.   Enterprise solutions contain the smallest amount of unique content.

      E.   An "enterprise solution" is an implementation of the enterprise architecture that provides the required business functions.

Q5:   Which of the following statements is not true?

      A.   The Enterprise Continuum should be interpreted as representing strictly chained relationships.

      B.   A populated Solutions Continuum can be regarded as a solutions inventory or re-use library.

      C.   Computer systems vendors are the primary provider of systems solutions.

      D.   An industry solution may include specific products, services, and systems solutions that are appropriate to that industry.

      E.   The primary purpose of connecting the Architecture Continuum to the Solutions Continuum is to build enterprise solutions on industry solutions, systems solutions, and products and services.

20.7 **Recommended Reading**

The following are recommended sources of further information for this chapter:

- TOGAF 8.1.1 Enterprise Edition Part III: Enterprise Continuum, Introduction to the Enterprise Continuum
- TOGAF 8.1.1 Enterprise Edition Part III: Enterprise Continuum, The Enterprise Continuum in Detail

PART 5

TOGAF and Other Architectures/Frameworks

Chapter 21

Positioning TOGAF

21.1 Key Learning Points

This chapter briefly describes TOGAF in relation to other frameworks.

Key Points Explained

This chapter will help you to answer the following questions:
- What examples of other frameworks are there and what are their main features?
- What is the difference between TOGAF and other architecture frameworks?
- What is the position of TOGAF in relation to other frameworks?

21.2 Positioning TOGAF

(Syllabus reference 5.1.1, 5.1.2)

TOGAF is one of a number of architectures and architecture frameworks in use today, many of which have a good deal in common with TOGAF.

The key points to stress when positioning TOGAF are as follows:
- The TOGAF ADM is a generic method.
- It is designed for use by enterprises in a wide variety of both geographies and industries.
- It can be tailored to meet specific needs.
- It can be used in conjunction with deliverables from another framework.
- A good example of its use with another framework is the Zachman Framework.

The following section provides examples of other frameworks, including information on their relationships to TOGAF.

21.3 Examples of Other Architectures and Frameworks

(Syllabus reference 5.1.2, 5.1.3)

Table 21-1 provides a summary of other architectures and frameworks described in TOGAF 8.1.1

Table 21.1: Summary of Other Architectures and Frameworks

Architecture/Framework	Owner	Summary
The C4ISR Architecture Framework	US Department of Defense	A comprehensive architecture guidance for the US Department of Defense Commands, Services, and Agencies. It has now evolved to become DODAF.
Common Object Request Broker Architecture (CORBA)	The Object Management Group	An object-oriented architecture that supports distributed computing and application integration.
Enterprise Architecture Planning (EAP)	Steven Spewak	A set of methods for planning the development of Information, Applications, and Technology Architectures and for aligning them with respect to each other.
The Practical Guide to Federal Enterprise Architecture	US Federal CIO Council	Guidance to US federal agencies in initiating, developing, using, and maintaining enterprise architectures.
The Federal Enterprise Architecture Framework (FEAF)	US Federal CIO Council	Direction and guidance to US federal agencies for structuring an enterprise architecture.
ISO/IEC 14252	ISO/IEC	An open systems architecture framework.
NCR Enterprise Architecture Framework	NCR	A computing architecture created to guide the development of systems, industry, and customer-specific architectures.
ISO Reference Model for Open Distributed Processing (RM-ODP)	ISO	A coordinating framework for standardization of open distributed processing.
Spirit Platform Blueprint	The Network Management Forum	A common, agreed set of specifications for a general-purpose computing platform.

Architecture/Framework	Owner	Summary
Technical Architecture Framework for Information Management (TAFIM)	US Department of Defense	The original framework on which TOGAF is based.
Treasury Enterprise Architecture Framework (TEAF)	US Department of the Treasury	Guidance for development and evolution of information systems architecture.
Zachman Framework	Zachman Institute of Framework Advancement	A framework providing a view of the subjects and models needed to develop a complete enterprise architecture.

A number of these are described in more detail in the following sections.

21.3.1 C4ISR Architecture Framework

C4ISR is an abbreviation for Command, Control, Computers, Communications, Intelligence, Surveillance, and Reconnaissance. The C4ISR Architecture Framework Version 2.0 is an architecture framework giving comprehensive guidance for these related US DoD domains. It was a successor to the Technical Architecture Framework for Information Management (TAFIM) and has subsequently been withdrawn and replaced by DODAF in 2003.

Relationship to TOGAF

Whereas the Architecture Development Method (ADM) forms a core part of TOGAF, guidance in the C4ISR Architecture Framework concerning the process of describing an architecture was intentionally kept to a minimum.

A major structural concept in the C4ISR Architecture Framework was the three sets of "views" (Operational, System, and Technical). Note that the use of the term "view" in the C4ISR Architecture Framework is different from the use of the term in TOGAF. DODAF has extended the views to add the "All" view that augments the other views by providing context, summary, or overview-level information, and an integrated dictionary to define terms.

21.3.2 Common Object Request Broker Architecture (CORBA)

The Object Management Group's (OMG) Object Management Architecture (OMA), often referred to as the CORBA architecture, is an object-oriented Applications Architecture based on the concept of an Object Request Broker

(ORB) (see www.omg.org/gettingstarted). The ORB acts as a switching center, locating objects, storing interface definitions and object implementations, and relaying messages between objects in a distributed heterogeneous environment.

Relationship to TOGAF

The CORBA architecture is an application-level architecture which focuses exclusively on issues affecting distributed object-oriented systems. It is consistent with TOGAF, and depends on the presence of lower-level facilities such as those described by TOGAF for operating system support, communications, and so on.

21.3.3 Enterprise Architecture Planning (EAP)

Steven Spewak's Enterprise Architecture Planning (EAP) is a set of methods for planning the development of Information, Applications, and Technology Architectures and for aligning the three types of architecture with respect to each other. The goal is to ensure that such architectures form the blueprints for sound, implementable systems that solve real business problems. The EAP methodology positions four types of "architecture" in the sequence: Business Architecture, Data Architecture, Applications Architecture, and Technology Architecture.

Relationship to TOGAF

The EAP methodology is analogous to the TOGAF ADM and can be mapped to it. However, EAP does not have a taxonomy of the various viewpoints and views, or a Foundation Architecture (Technical Reference Model (TRM) or Standards Information Base (SIB)).

21.3.4 Federal Enterprise Architecture: Practical Guide

The purpose of this document is to provide guidance to US federal agencies in initiating, developing, using, and maintaining their enterprise architectures. This guide offers an end-to-end process to initiate, implement, and sustain an enterprise architecture program, and describes the necessary roles and responsibilities for a successful enterprise architecture program.

Relationship to TOGAF

The Practical Guide's enterprise architecture processes closely align with the lifecycle phases of the TOGAF ADM. In addition, the Practical Guide adds steps such as establishing an enterprise architecture policy and establishing principles.

21.3.5   Federal Enterprise Architecture Framework (FEAF)

The FEAF promotes shared development for US federal processes, interoperability, and sharing of information among US federal agencies and other governmental entities. The FEAF provides direction and guidance to federal agencies for structuring an enterprise architecture.

Relationship to TOGAF

The FEAF contains guidance analogous to the TOGAF Foundation Architecture and architecture viewpoints and views.

21.3.6   ISO/IEC TR 14252 (IEEE Std 1003.0)

ISO/IEC TR 14252:1996, Guide to the POSIX Open System Environment is a direct line ancestor of TOGAF. TOGAF was originally based on TAFIM, which itself was a development of ISO/IEC TR 14252. It should be noted that the IEEE has administratively withdrawn the IEEE edition of this document

Relationship to TOGAF

At the topmost level they share a similar high-level reference model. ISO/IEC TR 14252 was the basis for the Technical Reference Model in TOGAF. TOGAF contains a considerable amount of material on architecture development that is lacking in ISO/IEC TR 14252.

21.3.7   ISO RM-ODP

RM-ODP provides a framework to support the development of standards that will support distributed processing in heterogeneous environments. It is based on the use of formal description techniques for specification of the architecture.

Relationship to TOGAF

RM-ODP is very tightly focused on problems relating to interactions between the objects making up distributed information processing systems, while TOGAF embraces the full spectrum of systems, whether distributed or not. As such, TOGAF coverage is a superset of that provided by RM-ODP. However, the relationship between the viewpoints described by RM-ODP and TOGAF's views is not an obvious one, and can be confusing.

21.3.8 SPIRIT Platform Blueprint Issue 3

SPIRIT is a joint effort between telecommunication service providers, computer system vendors, and independent software vendors, with the goal of producing a common, agreed set of specifications for a general-purpose computing platform.

Relationship to TOGAF

SPIRIT defines a practical, tested selection of specifications, most of which are referenced within the TOGAF Standards Information Base (SIB), that achieves portability and interoperability for largescale systems. The focus of SPIRIT is on ensuring that the SPIRIT selections are agreed by the vendor side for implementability and on the user side for procurability.

21.3.9 Technical Architecture Framework for Information Management (TAFIM)

TAFIM was developed from ISO/IEC TR 14252:1996, Guide to the POSIX Open System Environment (IEEE Std 1003.0), and was used as the basis of TOGAF Version 1. It was officially withdrawn in January 2000.

Relationship to TOGAF

TAFIM was the basis of TOGAF. The US Defense Information Systems Agency (DISA) contributed extensively to the development of TOGAF, and the two architecture frameworks have much in common. The TOGAF Technical Reference Model (TRM) was largely derived from TAFIM, and the TOGAF Architecture Development Method (ADM) was originally based on parts of TAFIM.

21.3.10 Zachman Framework

The Zachman Framework is a framework providing a view of the subjects and models needed to develop a complete enterprise architecture (see www.zifa.com). It is widely used for developing and/or documenting an enterprise-wide information systems architecture. Zachman based his framework on practices in traditional architecture and engineering. The purpose of the framework is to provide a basic structure which supports the organization, access, integration, interpretation, development, management, and changing of a set of architecture representations of the organization's information systems.

Relationship to TOGAF

The ADM mapping to the Zachman Framework supports a close correlation between the Zachman Framework and the TOGAF ADM. TOGAF can be used to populate the framework. The Zachman Framework provides a very comprehensive and well-established taxonomy of the various viewpoints, models, and other artifacts of an enterprise architecture. The viewpoints in TOGAF do not cover all of the Zachman Framework. However, with TOGAF it is possible to develop viewpoints and views to cover other aspects as necessary.

TOGAF recommends some viewpoints that are not included in the Zachman Framework; for example, the security and manageability viewpoints. The selection of viewpoints needs to be determined by the purpose of the architecture, and the TOGAF ADM defines a process for driving that selection. The vertical axis of the Zachman Framework provides a source of potential viewpoints for the architect to consider. The horizontal axis provides a generic taxonomy of concerns.

The Zachman Framework says nothing about the processes for developing viewpoints or conformant views, or the order in which they should be developed. It does not provide a method such as TOGAF's ADM, or a TRM or SIB. For more detailed information see TOGAF 8.1.1, Part IV: Resource Base, ADM and the Zachman Framework.

21.4 Summary

TOGAF is one of a number of architectures and architecture frameworks in use today, many of which are quite similar to TOGAF. One of the most important of these historically was TAFIM, as it was used as the basis of TOGAF Version 1. The TOGAF TRM was largely derived from TAFIM, and the ADM was originally based on parts of TAFIM.

The key points to stress when positioning TOGAF are as follows:
- The TOGAF ADM is a generic method.
- It is designed for use by enterprises in a wide variety of both geographies and industries.
- It can be tailored to meet specific needs.
- It can be used in conjunction with deliverables from another framework.

The Zachman Framework is a widely used approach for developing and/or documenting an enterprise-wide Information Systems Architecture and can be used in conjunction with TOGAF. Zachman based his framework on practices in traditional architecture and engineering. TOGAF can be used to populate the Zachman framework.

21.5 Test Yourself Questions

Q1:   TOGAF is one of a number of architectures and architecture frameworks in use today, many of which have a good deal in common with TOGAF. The following describe the positioning of TOGAF, except:

A.   TOGAF can be tailored to meet specific needs.
B.   The TOGAF ADM is a generic method.
C.   TOGAF is designed for use by enterprises in specific geographies and industries.
D.   TOGAF can be used in conjunction with deliverables from another framework.
E.   TOGAF can be used in conjunction with the Zachman Framework.

Q2:   Which of the following statements is not TRUE?

A.   The Zachman Framework is a widely used approach for developing and/or documenting an enterprise-wide Information Systems Architecture.
B.   The Zachman Framework is based on practices in traditional architecture and engineering.
C.   There is a close correlation between the Zachman Framework and the TOGAF ADM.
D.   The horizontal axis of the Zachman Framework provides a source of potential viewpoints for the architect to consider.
E.   The Zachman Framework says nothing about the process for developing viewpoints.

Q3:   Which of the following statements is not TRUE?

A.   C4ISR stands for Command, Control, Computers, Communications, Intelligence, Surveillance, and Reconnaissance.

B.   The CORBA architecture is an object-oriented Applications Architecture based on the concept of an Object Request Broker (ORB).

C.   Enterprise Architecture Planning (EAP) is a set of methods for planning the development of Information, Applications, and Technology Architectures and for aligning the three types of architecture with respect to each other.

D.   The purpose of the Federal Enterprise Architecture: Practical Guide is to provide guidance to US federal agencies in initiating, developing, using, and maintaining their enterprise architectures.

E.   The TOGAF Architecture Development Method (ADM) was originally based on parts of SPIRIT.

Q4:   Which of the following statements is not TRUE?
A.   EAP has a taxonomy of viewpoints and views.
B.   The FEAF contains guidance analogous to the TOGAF Foundation Architecture and architecture viewpoints and views.
C.   TOGAF coverage is a superset of that provided by RM-ODP.
D.   SPIRIT defines a practical, tested selection of specifications, most of which are referenced within the TOGAF (SIB).
E.   The Zachman framework does not provide a method such as TOGAF's ADM, or a TRM or SIB.

Q5:   Which of the following statements is not TRUE?
A.   The use of the term "view" in the C4ISR Architecture Framework is different from the use of the term in TOGAF.
B.   CORBA focuses exclusively on issues affecting distributed object-oriented systems.
C.   The EAP methodology is analogous to the TOGAF ADM.
D.   TAFIM and TOGAF have very little in common.
E.   The viewpoints in TOGAF do not cover all of the Zachman Framework.

Q6:   The US DoD C4ISR Architecture Framework provides three views. Which of the following sets of views is provided?
A.   Logical, physical, system
B.   Technical, physical, logical
C.   Operational, system, technical

D.   Logical, operational, system

E.   Technical, physical, operational

21.6 Recommended Reading

The following are recommended sources of further information for this chapter:

- TOGAF 8.1.1 Enterprise Edition Part IV: Resource Base, Other Architectures and Frameworks
- TOGAF 8.1.1 Enterprise Edition Part IV: Resource Base, ADM and the Zachman Framework

PART 6

Architecture Governance

Chapter 22

Architecture Governance

22.1 Key Learning Points

Architecture governance is the practice and orientation by which enterprise architectures and other architectures are managed and controlled.

Key Points Explained

This chapter will help you to answer the following questions:
- What is architecture governance?
- What are the main concepts that make up an Architecture Governance Framework?
- Why is architecture governance beneficial?

22.2 Introduction to Governance

22.2.1 Nature of Governance

(Syllabus reference 6.1.1)

Governance is essentially about ensuring that business is conducted properly. It is less about overt control and strict adherence to rules, and more about effective usage of resources to ensure sustainability of an organization's strategic objectives.

22.2.2 Levels of Governance

(Syllabus reference 6.1.2)

Architecture governance is the practice and orientation by which enterprise architectures and other architectures are managed and controlled at an enterprise-wide level.

Architecture governance typically does not operate in isolation, but within a hierarchy of governance structures which, particularly in the larger enterprise, can include the following as distinct domains with their own disciplines and processes: corporate governance, technology governance, IT governance, and architecture governance. Each of these domains of governance may exist at multiple geographic levels – global, regional, and local – within the overall enterprise. Corporate governance is a broad topic and outside the scope of the TOGAF framework.

22.3 TOGAF Architecture Governance Framework
(Syllabus reference 6.2)

Phase G of the TOGAF ADM is dedicated to implementation governance, which concerns itself with the realization of the architecture through change projects. Architecture governance covers the management and control of all aspects of the development and evolution of architectures. It needs to be supported by an Architecture Governance Framework which assists in identifying effective processes so that the business responsibilities associated with architecture governance can be elucidated, communicated, and managed effectively. TOGAF provides such a framework.

22.3.1 Conceptual Structure
(Syllabus reference 6.2.1)

Architecture governance is an approach, a series of processes, a cultural orientation, and set of owned responsibilities that ensure the integrity and effectiveness of the organization's architectures. The key concepts are shown in Figure 22-1.

The split of process, content, and context is key to supporting an architecture governance initiative. It allows the introduction of new governance material (for example, due to new regulations) without unduly impacting the processes. The content-agnostic approach ensures the framework is flexible.

22.3.1.1 Key Architecture Governance Processes
There are six processes that are key:
1. Policy Management and Take-On
2. Compliance
3. Dispensation
4. Monitoring and Reporting

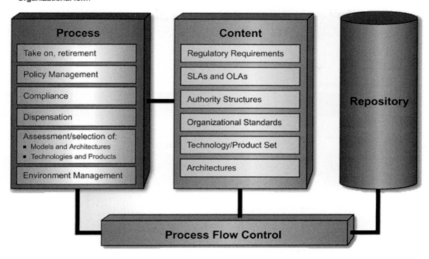

Context
Drivers (industry, regulatory, political, legislative, legal)
Organizational form

Figure 22.1: Architecture Governance Framework – Conceptual Structure

5. Business Control
6. Environment Management

22.3.2 Organizational Structure
(Syllabus reference 6.2.2)

Governance is the practice of managing and controlling architectures. An effective architecture governance structure requires processes, structures, and capabilities (see Figure 22-2) and will typically include a global governance board, local governance board, design authorities, and working parties.

Architecture governance is beneficial because it:
- Links IT processes, resources, and information to organizational strategies and objectives
- Integrates and institutionalizes IT best practices
- Aligns with industry frameworks such as COBIT (planning and organizing, acquiring and implementing, delivering and supporting, and monitoring IT performance)
- Enables the organization to take full advantage of its information, infrastructure, and hardware and software assets

- Protects the underlying digital assets of the organization
- Supports regulatory and best practice requirements such as auditability, security, responsibility, and accountability
- Promotes visible risk management

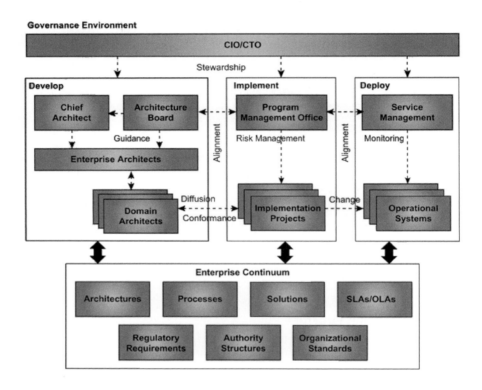

Figure 22.2: Architecture Governance Framework – Organizational Structure

22.4 Architecture Governance in Practice
(Syllabus reference 6.3)

22.4.1 Key Success Factors

It is important to consider the following to ensure a successful approach to architecture governance, and effective management of the Architecture Contract:

- Establishment and operation of best practices for submission, adoption, re-use, reporting, and retirement of architecture policies, procedures, roles, skills, organizational structures, and support services

- Establishment of correct organizational responsibilities and structures to support architecture governance processes and reporting requirements
- Integration of tools and processes to facilitate take-up of processes (both procedural and cultural take-up)
- Management of criteria for control of architecture governance processes, dispensations, compliance assessments, Service Level Agreements (SLAs), and Operational Level Agreements (OLAs)
- Meeting internal and external requirements for effectiveness, efficiency, confidentiality, integrity, availability, compliance, and reliability of architecture governance-related information, services, and processes

22.4.2 Architecture Board
(Syllabus reference 6.3.1)

A cross-organizational Architecture Board must be established with the backing of top management to oversee the implementation of the IT governance strategy (see Section 15.2.4). The Architecture Board is typically made responsible, and accountable, for achieving some or all of the following goals:
- Consistency between sub-architectures
- Identifying re-usable components
- Flexibility of enterprise architecture; to meet business needs and utilize new technologies
- Enforcement of Architecture Compliance
- Improving the maturity level of architecture discipline within the organization
- Ensuring that the discipline of architecture-based development is adopted
- Providing the basis for all decision-making with regard to changes to the architectures
- Supporting a visible escalation capability for out-of-bounds decisions

The Architecture Board is also responsible for operational items such as the monitoring and control of Architecture Contracts, and for governance items such as producing usable governance materials. See TOGAF 8.1.1, Part IV: Resource Base, Architecture Board for more information.

22.4.3 Architecture Compliance
(Syllabus reference 6.3.2)

Ensuring the compliance of individual projects within the enterprise
architecture is an essential aspect of architecture governance. An Architecture
Compliance strategy should be adopted. Specific measures are needed
to ensure compliance with the architecture, including Project Impact
Assessments and a formal Architecture Compliance Review process.

Project Impact Assessments are prepared by the architecture function and
are project-specific views of the enterprise architecture that illustrate how the
enterprise architecture impacts on the major projects within an organization.

The Architecture Compliance Review process is a formal process for
reviewing the compliance of projects to the enterprise architecture. The
TOGAF document includes a detailed process and checklists for this process.

22.4.4 Architecture Contracts
(Syllabus reference 6.3.3)

Architecture Contracts (see Section 15.2.26) are joint agreements between
development partners and sponsors on the deliverables, quality, and
fitness-for-purpose of an architecture. Successful implementation of these
agreements will be delivered through effective architecture governance.
Taking a governed approach to contract management ensures a system
of continuous monitoring of integrity, changes, decision-making, and
audit, as well as adherence to the principles, standards, and requirements
of the enterprise. The architecture team may also be included in product
procurement, to help minimize the opportunity for misinterpretation of the
enterprise architecture.

22.5 Summary

Architecture governance is the practice and orientation by which enterprise
architectures and other architectures are managed and controlled at an
enterprise-wide level. It includes the following:
* Implementing a system of controls over the creation and monitoring
  of all architecture components and activities, to ensure the effective

introduction, implementation, and evolution of architectures within the organization

- Implementing a system to ensure compliance with internal and external standards and regulatory obligations
- Establishing processes that support effective management of the above processes within agreed parameters
- Developing practices that ensure accountability to a clearly identified stakeholder community, both inside and outside the organization

22.6 Test Yourself Questions

Q1: Which of the following statements about architecture governance is not true?

A. It is the practice and orientation by which enterprise architectures and other architectures are managed and controlled.

B. The CEO manages the architecture governance activity.

C. A governance board manages the architecture governance activity.

D. An Architecture Governance Framework supports it.

E. It is set of owned responsibilities that ensure the integrity and effectiveness of the organization's architecture.

Q2: The following are included in Architecture Governance, except:

A. Implementing a system of controls over expenditure within the enterprise

B. Implementing a system of controls over the creation and monitoring of all architecture components and activities

C. Implementing a system to ensure compliance with internal and external standards and regulatory obligations

D. Establishing processes that support effective management of the architecture governance process

E. Developing practices that ensure accountability to stakeholders

Q3: Which of the following maps to the characteristic "transparency"?

A. All decisions taken, processes used, and their implementation will not be allowed to create unfair advantage to any one particular party.

B. Each contractual party is required to act responsibly to the organization and its shareholders.

    C.   All actions implemented and their decision support will be available for inspection by authorized organization and provider parties.

    D.   All involved parties will have a commitment to adhere to procedures, processes, and authority structures established by the organization.

    E.   All processes, decision-making, and mechanisms used will be established so as to minimize or avoid potential conflicts of interest.

Q4:   Which of the following lists the governance structures into a hierarchy with the broadest applicability given last?

    A.   Corporate governance, IT governance, technology governance, architecture governance

    B.   IT governance, technology governance, architecture governance, IT governance

    C.   Technology governance, architecture governance, IT governance, corporate governance

    D.   Architecture governance, IT governance, technology governance, corporate governance

    E.   IT governance, corporate governance, architecture governance, technology governance

Q5:   Conceptually, the structure of an Architecture Governance Framework consists of Process, Content, and Context (stored in the repository). The following are included in Content, except:

    A.   Compliance

    B.   SLAs and OLAs

    C.   Organizational Standards

    D.   Regulatory Requirements

    E.   Architectures

Q6:   The following are key architecture governance processes, except:

    A.   Compliance

    B.   Dispensation

    C.   Monitoring and Reporting

    D.   Budgetary Control

    E.   Business Control

Q7:   Establishing an Architecture Board prevents one-off solutions and
      unconstrained developments that lead to:
      A.   High costs of development
      B.   High costs of support
      C.   Lower quality
      D.   Numerous run-time environments
      E.   All of these

Q8:   Why is architecture governance beneficial?
      A.   It links IT processes, resources, and information to organizational
           strategies and objectives.
      B.   It integrates and institutionalizes IT best practices.
      C.   It enables the organization to take full advantage of its
           information, infrastructure, and hardware and software assets.
      D.   It protects the underlying digital assets of the organization.
      E.   All of these

Q9:   Which of the following is an example of an IT governance framework?
      A.   ITIL
      B.   PRINCE 2
      C.   COBIT
      D.   TOGAF
      E.   ATAM

Q10: Which of the following is not a key architecture governance process?
      A.   Undertaking compliance assessments against SLAs
      B.   Architecture implementation
      C.   Granting dispensations
      D.   Business control to ensure compliance with business policies
      E.   Managing architecture amendments, contracts, etc.

Q11: The following management guidelines are built into COBIT, except:
      A.   Maturity models
      B.   Critical success factors
      C.   Key goal indicators
      D.   Service level agreements
      E.   Key performance indicators

22.7 Recommended Reading

The following are recommended sources of further information for this chapter:

- TOGAF 8.1.1 Enterprise Edition Part IV: Resource Base, Architecture Board
- TOGAF 8.1.1 Enterprise Edition Part IV: Resource Base, Architecture Compliance
- TOGAF 8.1.1 Enterprise Edition Part IV: Resource Base, Architecture Governance

Answers to Test Yourself Questions

A.1 Answers to the Test Yourself Questions

This appendix contains a table of the answers to the Test Yourself Questions and has a cell corresponding to each chapter of the Study Guide.

Reference	Answer	Notes
Chapter 1	Q1. B	There are four classes: TOGAF Certified, TOGAF Training, TOGAF Tool Support, TOGAF Professional Services.
	Q2. A	TOGAF 8 Certified is for individuals.
	Q3. B	TOGAF Training is for course materials.
	Q4. C	The goals of the program include integrity, objectivity, and scalability.
	Q5. D	
	Q6. E	
Chapter 2	Q1. B	
	Q2. E	
	Q3. C	The TRM, is part of the Foundation Architecture.
	Q4. E	
	Q5. D	
Chapter 3	Q1. A	
	Q2. D	
	Q3. B	It should be Phase B: Business Architecture.
	Q4. E	
	Q5. C	
	Q6. B	
	Q7. B	
Chapter 4	Q1. A	
	Q2. E	
	Q3. A	
	Q4. B	
	Q5. D	
	Q6. D	

Reference	Answer	Notes
Chapter 5	Q1. E	
	Q2. B	
	Q3. C	
	Q4. D	
	Q5. E	
	Q6. B	
	Q7. C	
Chapter 6	Q1. E	
	Q2. B	
	Q3. A	
	Q4. E	
	Q5. C	
Chapter 7	Q1. B	
	Q2. E	
	Q3. C	
Chapter 8	Q1. C	
	Q2. B	
	Q3. D	
	Q4. E	
	Q5. A	
Chapter 9	Q1. B	
	Q2. B	
	Q3. D	
	Q4. B	
	Q5. C	
Chapter 10	Q1. B	
	Q2. D	
	Q3. E	
	Q4. E	
	Q5. C	
Chapter 11	Q1. A	
	Q2. D	
	Q3. B	
	Q4. D	
	Q5. B	
	Q6. D	
	Q7. B	

Reference	Answer	Notes
Chapter 12	Q1. E	
	Q2. D	
	Q3. B	
	Q4. A	
	Q5. E	
Chapter 13	Q1. D	
	Q2. D	
	Q3. A	
Chapter 14	Q1. D	
	Q2. B	
	Q3. D	
	Q4. E	
	Q5. C	
Chapter 15	Q1. E	
	Q2. C	
	Q3. D	
	Q4. E	Since it is an Application Principle.
	Q5. B	
	Q6. C	
	Q7. B	
	Q8. C	
	Q9. B	
	Q10. B	
	Q11. A	
	Q12. D	
	Q13. B	
	Q14. C	
	Q15. B	
	Q16. A	
	Q17. B	
	Q18. D	
	Q19. E	
	Q20. E	

Reference	Answer	Notes
Chapter 16	Q1. D	
	Q2. B	
	Q3. C	
	Q4. D	
	Q5. B	
	Q6. E	
Chapter 17	Q1. A	
	Q2. A	
	Q3. D	
	Q4. E	
	Q5. E	Note non-current standards have a status of obsolete that is still adopted.
	Q6. D	The SIB is an input to the steps within the Technology Phase.
Chapter 18	Q1. A	
	Q2. A	
	Q3. E	
	Q4. B	
	Q5. E	
Chapter 19	Q1. E	
	Q2. B	
	Q3. E	
	Q4. A	
	Q5. B	
Chapter 20	Q1. B	
	Q2. A	
	Q3. E	
	Q4. D	
	Q5. A	
Chapter 21	Q1. C	
	Q2. D	
	Q3. E	
	Q4. A	
	Q5. D	
	Q6. C	

Reference	Answer	Notes
Chapter 22	Q1. B	
	Q2. A	
	Q3. C	
	Q4. D	
	Q5. A	
	Q6. D	
	Q7. E	
	Q8. E	
	Q9. C	
	Q10. B	
	Q11. D	

Test Yourself Examination Paper

B.1 Examination Paper

The purpose of this appendix is to provide an examination paper that will allow you to assess your knowledge of TOGAF 8.1.1.

Prior to attempting this examination paper you should have worked through this Study Guide section by section, answering the test yourself questions and reading the referenced sections from the TOGAF document. If you have completed your preparation, then you can then attempt this examination paper. If not, please spend some time preparing as suggested.

B.2 Questions

The examination paper provided in this appendix uses an extended multiple-choice format asking you to select true or false to a number of statements in each knowledge area, whereas the actual examination requires one correct answer from five. This paper is designed to give a thorough test of your knowledge to enable you to assess your readiness to take the real examination.

Introduction to TOGAF

1: The ADM is a generic method for architecture development designed to deal with most system and organizational requirements. Indicate whether the following statements are TRUE or FALSE.

    a. The order of the phases in the ADM is independent of the maturity of the architecture discipline within the enterprise.

    b. It is impossible to integrate TOGAF with the Zachman Framework.

    c. The ADM can be used as a general program management method.

    d. A complete architecture should address four domains (Business, Data, Applications, Technology).

    e. The order of the phases in the ADM may be defined by the business and architecture principles of an enterprise.

2: Largescale architectures are often undertaken in the form of "federated architectures". Indicate whether the following statements are TRUE or FALSE.

   a. Complex architectures are hard to manage.

   b. One approach to federated architecture development is to divide the enterprise up "vertically" into "segments" each representing a business sector within the enterprise.

   c. The approach known as "super-domains" divides an enterprise architecture horizontally so that each architecture domain (Business, Data, Applications, and Technology) covers the full extent of the enterprise.

   d. "Super-domain" architectures projects are usually undertaken as integrated projects, with the same personnel.

   e. The US Federal CIO Council chose the "segment" approach in its Federal Enterprise Architecture Framework.

Phase A: Architecture Vision

3: The Architecture Vision is an opportunity to sell the benefits of the proposed development within an enterprise. Indicate whether the following statements are TRUE or FALSE.

   a. Clarifying and agreeing on the purpose of the architecture effort is one of the key parts of this activity.

   b. Key elements of the Architecture Vision include the enterprise mission, vision, strategy, and business case.

   c. The Architecture Vision includes a high-level description of the baseline and target environments.

   d. Business scenarios are an appropriate technique to discover and document business requirements.

   e. Once an Architecture Vision is defined and documented it is not necessary to use it to build a consensus.

4: It is important to define the scope of the architecture effort. Indicate whether the following statements are TRUE or FALSE.

   a. Scope includes the level of detail to be defined.

   b. Scope includes the specific architecture domains to be covered (Business, Data, Applications, Technology).

   c. Scope does not include the extent of the time horizon.

   d. Scope includes assets created in previous iterations of the ADM cycle.

   e. Scope does not include assets available elsewhere in the industry.

Stakeholders and Concerns, Business Requirements, and Architecture Vision

5: Key stakeholders must be identified. Indicate whether the following statements are TRUE or FALSE.

   a. Business scenarios are an appropriate technique to articulate an Architecture Vision.

   b. Human actors do not need to be identified.

   c. Objectives and measures of success should be identified.

   d. Computer actors do not need to be identified.

   e. Roles and responsibilities should be identified.

Development of a Business Architecture

6: The Business Architecture is the first architecture activity that needs to be undertaken. Indicate whether the following statements are TRUE or FALSE.

   a. The Business Architecture is often necessary to show the business value of subsequent Technology Architecture work to key stakeholders.

   b. Key elements of the Business Architecture may be done in other activities.

   c. The business strategy typically defines what to achieve and how to get there.

   d. A key objective is to re-use existing material as much as possible.

   e. Phase B will rarely involve a lot of detailed work.

7: An objective of Phase B is to describe the Baseline Business Architecture and a Target Business Architecture. Indicate whether the following statements are TRUE or FALSE.

   a. The normal approach to Target Architecture development is top-down.

   b. The analysis of the Baseline Architecture often has to be done top-down.

   c. Business process models describe the functions associated with the business, the internal data exchanges, and the external data exchanges.

   d. A use-case model describes business processes in terms of use-cases and actors.

   e. A class model describes dynamic information and relationships between information.

Business Modeling and Business Models

8: A variety of modeling tools and techniques can be used to model a business. Indicate which of the following statements are TRUE or FALSE.
    a. Activity models capture the activities performed in a business process together with the inputs, controls, outputs, and resources used.
    b. Activity models and use-case models can be represented in Unified Modeling Language, but class models cannot.
    c. Node connectivity within a Node Connectivity Diagram can be described at three levels: conceptual, logical, physical.
    d. RosettaNet is a consortium that has developed a set of e-business processes for supply chain use.
    e. Generic business models relevant to an organization's industry sector are termed "Common Systems Architectures" in the Enterprise Continuum.

Gap Analysis

9: A key step in validating an architecture is to consider what may have been forgotten. Indicate whether the following statements are TRUE or FALSE.
    a. Gaps are not usually found by considering stakeholder concerns.
    b. Gaps are not usually found by considering buildings and office space.
    c. Duplicate or missing tool functionality should be considered.
    d. Cross-training requirements should be considered.
    e. Process inefficiencies should not be considered.

Views

10: A view is a representation of a whole system from the perspective of a related set of concerns. Indicate whether the following statements are TRUE or FALSE.
    a. A possible Business Architecture view is the usability view.
    b. A logical data view can be part of a Data Architecture view.
    c. A software engineering view is usually part of a Technology Architecture view.
    d. A hardware view is not usually part of a Technology Architecture view.
    e. A data flow view is usually part of a Data Architecture view.

Viewpoints

11: A viewpoint defines the perspective from which a view is taken. Indicate whether the following statements are TRUE or FALSE.

   a. Viewpoints are generic and can be stored in libraries for re-use.
   b. Every view has an associated viewpoint that describes it, at least implicitly.
   c. A viewpoint is not normally developed or visualized using a tool.
   d. Relevant Business Architecture viewpoints include operational, managerial, and financial.
   e. A viewpoint does not define how to construct or use a view.

Business Architecture Model

12: An objective of Phase B is to develop a Target Business Architecture. Indicate whether the following statements are TRUE or FALSE.

   a. It is important to create a model of the organization structure.
   b. It is important to model the business goals and objectives.
   c. It is not necessary to include measures and deliverables when modeling the business processes.
   d. It is necessary to relate business functions to organizational units in the form of a matrix report.
   e. Gap analysis should be used to resolve conflicts.

Information Systems Architectures

13: The objective of Phase C is to develop Target Architectures covering the Data and/or Applications Architecture domains. Indicate whether the following statements are TRUE or FALSE.

   a. A common implementation approach is bottom-up design and top-down implementation.
   b. The Data Architecture is usually developed before the Applications Architecture.
   c. Gap analysis can be used to find omissions in data services and/or data elements.
   d. Entity-relationship diagrams can be used in the Baseline Data Architecture description.
   e. Logical data models are rarely used in the Baseline Data Architecture description.

Data Architecture

14: The objective of the Data Architecture is to define the major types and sources of data necessary to support the business. Indicate whether the following statements are TRUE or FALSE.

   a. Data entities in the Data Architecture should be mapped to business functions in the Business Architecture.

   b. It is important to indicate which of the CRUD operations are performed by which functions.

   c. Impact Analysis is used to resolve conflicts among the different views.

   d. Non-functional requirements are not usually reviewed during Data Architecture development.

   e. A formal checkpoint review of the architecture model and building blocks is unnecessary.

Applications Architecture

15: The objective of the Applications Architecture is to define the major kinds of application system necessary to process the data and support the business. Indicate whether the following statements are TRUE or FALSE.

   a. It is important to model at least the Common Applications Services view and the Applications Interoperability view.

   b. Potential application systems can be found by brainstorming.

   c. The Applications Architecture document does not need to be reviewed by stakeholders.

   d. A gap analysis should be performed to identify any areas where the Business Architecture may need to change.

   e. Qualitative criteria should be reviewed.

Technology Architecture

16: The objective of Phase D is to develop a Technology Architecture for implementation. Indicate whether the following statements are TRUE or FALSE.

   a. It is not necessary to develop a Baseline Description of the existing Technology Architecture.

   b. The Business Architecture is used to select the most relevant viewpoints for the project.

   c. Views to consider include Hardware, Communications, Processing, Cost, and Standards.

    d. Impact Analysis should be used to resolve conflicts among the different viewpoints.

    e. The Technology Architecture model usually starts as a TOGAF TRM-based model.

17: Outputs from previous phases are used in Phase D. Indicate whether the following statements are TRUE or FALSE.

    a. Technology principles are used as inputs to Phase D if they exist.

    b. The Statement of Architecture Work is used as an input to Phase D.

    c. The Architecture Vision is not used as an input to Phase D.

    d. Relevant technical requirements from previous phases are used as inputs to Phase D.

    e. The gap analysis from the Data Architecture is used as an input to Phase D.

18: Phase D includes the development of the Baseline Technology Architecture description. Indicate whether the following statements are TRUE or FALSE.

    a. The scope and level of detail for the Baseline Description of the existing Technology Architecture depends on the extent to which existing technology components will be re-used.

    b. The Baseline Description should include a plain language description of what each hardware platform is and what it is used for.

    c. The networks accessed are not included in the Baseline Description.

    d. Graphics and schematics should be used to illustrate baseline configuration(s).

    e. The Baseline Technology Architecture Report is not usually sent for review by relevant stakeholders.

19: During Phase D the Target Technology Architecture is developed. Indicate whether the following statements are TRUE or FALSE.

    a. The objective of this step is to convert the description of the existing system into services terminology using the organization's Foundation Architecture.

    b. The TOGAF Foundation Architecture's TRM can be used.

    c. The conceptualization of Architecture Building Blocks should have been done in a previous phase.

    d. Architecture Building Blocks are intended to be solutions.

    e. An architecture description language can be used to document the Architecture Building Blocks.

20: The first step of the Target Technology Architecture development is to create a Baseline Description in the TOGAF format. Indicate whether the following statements are TRUE or FALSE.

   a. The objective of this step is to convert the description of the existing system into object-oriented terminology.

   b. This step captures candidates for re-usable building blocks from the existing architecture.

   c. An important task is to set down a list of key questions that can be used later to measure the effectiveness of the new architecture.

   d. It is not necessary to review and validate the set of Technology Architecture principles during this step.

   e. It is not necessary to verify the Technology Architecture model during this step.

21: The second step of the Target Technology Architecture development is to consider different architecture reference models, viewpoints, and tools. Indicate whether the following statements are TRUE or FALSE.

   a. The objectives of this step are to perform an analysis of the Technology Architecture from a number of different viewpoints and to document each relevant viewpoint.

   b. The Data Architecture is used to select the most relevant viewpoints for the project.

   c. A comprehensive set of stakeholder viewpoints must be created for the target system.

   d. Views to consider include Hardware, Communications, Processing, Cost, and Database.

   e. Sophisticated modeling tools and techniques must be used when modeling and analyzing the Target Technology Architecture in association with the selected viewpoints.

22: The third step of the Target Technology Architecture development is to create an architecture model of building blocks. Indicate whether the following statements are TRUE or FALSE.

   a. An architecture based exactly on the TOGAF TRM may not be able to accommodate the stakeholder needs of all organizations.

   b. It is not possible to make decisions about how the various elements of system functionality should be implemented in this step.

   c. This step defines the future model of Architecture Building Blocks.

    d. The model is not usually tested for coverage and completeness of the required technical functions.

    e. An input to this step is the Architecture Vision.

23: The fourth step of the Target Technology Architecture development is to select the services portfolio required for each building block. Indicate whether the following statements are TRUE or FALSE.

    a. Some of the services in the service description portfolio may be conflicting.

    b. One of the inputs to Step 4 is the Technical Reference Model (TRM).

    c. One of the inputs to Step 4 is the Standards Information Base (SIB).

    d. One of the inputs to Step 4 is the Data Architecture.

    e. A key activity in Step 4 is producing a list of services arranged alphabetically.

24: The fifth step of the Target Technology Architecture development is to confirm that the business goals and objectives are met. Indicate whether the following statements are TRUE or FALSE.

    a. One of the inputs to this step is the Business Architecture.

    b. One of the inputs to this step is the Applications Architecture.

    c. A key activity in this step is to perform an Impact Analysis using the specifications and portfolios of specifications.

    d. One of the key activities in this step is a formal checkpoint review of the architecture model and building blocks.

    e. One of the key activities in this step is validating that business goals are met.

25: The sixth step of the Target Technology Architecture development is to develop a set of criteria for choosing specifications and portfolios of specifications. Indicate whether the following statements are TRUE or FALSE.

    a. Large organizations often consider the most important criteria to be a high level of consensus.

    b. A key activity in this step is to brainstorm criteria for choosing specifications and portfolios of specifications.

    c. A key activity in this step is to perform an Impact Analysis using the specifications and portfolios of specifications.

    d. One of the inputs to this step is the Architecture Vision.

    e. One of the outputs of this step is the Applications Architecture.

26: The seventh step of the Target Technology Architecture development is to complete the architecture definition. Indicate whether the following statements are TRUE or FALSE.

   a. The objective of this step is to fully specify the Applications Architecture.
   b. The selection of building blocks and interfaces only has a small impact on how the original requirements are met.
   c. The specification of building blocks as a portfolio of services is an evolutionary process.
   d. The earliest building block definitions start as relatively abstract.
   e. One of the inputs to this step is the Data Architecture.

27: There are a number of key activities in Step 7 of the Target Technology Architecture development. Indicate whether the following statements are TRUE or FALSE.

   a. A key activity in this step is to select standards for each of the Architecture Building Blocks.
   b. A key activity in this step is to document the final mapping of the architecture within the Architecture Continuum.
   c. A key activity in this step is to document the rationale for building block decisions.
   d. A key activity in this step is to present the current state of the architecture to sponsors in order to negotiate a continuation.
   e. A key activity in this step is to ensure that the Business Architecture remains unchanged.

Phase E: Opportunities and Solutions

28: Phase E is concerned with opportunities and solutions for implementation. Indicate whether the following statements are TRUE or FALSE.

   a. One of the objectives of Phase E is to evaluate and select suitable Architecture Building Blocks.
   b. One of the objectives of Phase E is to assess the dependencies, costs, and benefits of the various projects.
   c. It is never necessary to iterate between Phase E and previous phases.
   d. Phase E is the first phase which is directly concerned with implementation.
   e. Trade-off analysis is an effective approach for this phase.

29: Phase E continued. Indicate whether the following statements are TRUE or FALSE.
   a. Coexistence of the old and new systems is straightforward.
   b. Projects that deliver short-term pay-offs should be given low priority.
   c. One of the inputs to this phase is the Architecture Vision.
   d. One of the inputs to this phase is the Request for Architecture Work.
   e. One of the inputs to this phase is the Business Architecture.

30: Phase E continued. Indicate whether the following statements are TRUE or FALSE.
   a. A key step in Phase E is to brainstorm technical requirements from a functional perspective.
   b. A key step in Phase E is to brainstorm co-existence and interoperability requirements.
   c. A key step in Phase E is to perform a requirements analysis.
   d. One of the outputs from this phase is a trade-off analysis.
   e. One of the outputs from this phase is a list of re-usable Architecture Building Blocks.

Phase F: Migration Planning

31: Phase F is concerned with migration planning. Indicate whether the following statements are TRUE or FALSE.
   a. The objective of Phase F is to sort the various implementation projects into alphabetical order.
   b. An important consideration is the cost of retraining the users.
   c. An important consideration is the likely cultural impact on the user community.
   d. Migration rarely requires consideration of technical issues.
   e. The most successful basic strategy is to focus on the most complex projects first.

32: Phase F continued. Indicate whether the following statements are TRUE or FALSE.
   a. Distributed systems can be treated in the same way as non-distributed systems.
   b. A common approach is to implement business functions in a data-driven chronological sequence.
   c. One of the inputs to Phase F is the Data Architecture.
   d. One of the inputs to Phase F is the Business Architecture.
   e. One of the inputs to Phase F is an Impact Analysis project list.

33: Phase F continued. Indicate whether the following statements are TRUE or FALSE.
   a. A key step in Phase F is to list the projects in alphabetical order.
   b. A key step in Phase F is to estimate resource requirements and availability.
   c. A key step in Phase F is to perform risk assessment.
   d. A key step in Phase F is a cost/benefit assessment of the migration projects.
   e. The output of Phase F is a gap analysis.

Phase G: Implementation Governance

34: Phase G is concerned with Implementation Governance. Indicate whether the following statements are TRUE or FALSE.
   a. One of the objectives of Phase G is to formulate recommendations for each implementation project.
   b. One of the objectives of Phase G is to perform appropriate governance functions while the system is being implemented.
   c. The actual development happens when Phase G has finished.
   d. One of the inputs to Phase G is the Data Architecture.
   e. One of the inputs to Phase G is the set of Architecture Building Blocks.

35: Phase G continued. Indicate whether the following statements are TRUE or FALSE.
   a. A key step in Phase G is documenting the scope of the individual projects.
   b. A key step in Phase G is obtaining signatures from all developing organizations.
   c. A key step in Phase G is a gap analysis.
   d. One of the outputs from Phase G is an Architecture Contract.
   e. One of the outputs from Phase G is a gap analysis.

Phase H: Architecture Change Management

36: Phase H is concerned with establishing procedures for managing change. Indicate whether the following statements are TRUE or FALSE.
   a. Phase H will typically provide for the continual monitoring of new developments in technology.
   b. A goal of this phase is to ensure that the enterprise architecture is not permitted to change.

c. A goal of this phase is to ensure that the enterprise architecture development cycle does not restart.

d. The governance body must establish criteria to judge whether a change request warrants merely an architecture update or a new cycle of the ADM.

e. Guidelines for establishing criteria are straightforward to prescribe.

37: Phase H continued. Indicate whether the following statements are TRUE or FALSE.

a. Technology-related drivers for architecture change include new technology reports.

b. Technology-related drivers for architecture change include asset management cost reductions.

c. PRINCE 2 is a project management method that can be used in this phase.

d. The three categories of architecture change are Simplification, Incremental, and Prototyping.

e. If a change impacts two stakeholders then it is likely to be a candidate for change management.

38: Phase H continued. Indicate whether the following statements are TRUE or FALSE.

a. Ten systems reduced or changed to one system would be classed as an incremental change.

b. One of the inputs to Phase H is the set of Architecture Building Blocks.

c. One of the inputs to Phase H is the set of standards initiatives.

d. A key step in Phase H is the meeting of the Architecture Board (or other governing council).

e. One of the outputs from Phase H is a list of prioritized projects.

ADM Architecture Requirements Management

39: Architecture requirements must be managed throughout the ADM. Indicate whether the following statements are TRUE or FALSE.

a. TOGAF does not mandate or recommend a specific process or tool for requirements management.

b. The Volère Requirements Specification Template may be of use.

c. The inputs to the Requirements Management process are the requirements-related outputs from each ADM phase.

d. The output of the Requirements Management process itself is the System Requirements Specification.

e. Determining stakeholder satisfaction with the decisions is optional.

ADM Input and Output Descriptions

Major Input Descriptions

40: The Architecture Development Method requires and provides a number of inputs and outputs. Indicate whether the following statements are TRUE or FALSE.

a. One of the inputs to the Request for Architecture Work is the organization's mission statement.

b. One of the inputs to the Request for Architecture Work is the set of strategic plans for the business.

c. One of the inputs to the Request for Architecture Work is the list of new developments in potentially relevant technologies.

d. Budget information is not needed as an input to the Request for Architecture Work.

e. Organizational constraints are not needed as an input to the Request for Architecture Work.

Major Output Descriptions

41: The Architecture Development Method inputs and outputs continued. Indicate whether the following statements are TRUE or FALSE.

a. One of the outputs of the Statement of Architecture Work is the Architecture Vision.

b. One of the outputs of the Statement of Architecture Work is a set of signature approvals.

c. One of the outputs of the Business Architecture is the problem description.

d. One of the outputs of the Business Architecture is the set of actors together with their roles and responsibilities.

e. One of the outputs of the Business Architecture is the set of relevant business process descriptions.

42: The Architecture Development Method inputs and outputs continued. Indicate whether the following statements are TRUE or FALSE.

a. One of the outputs of the Technology Architecture is a set of Architecture Building Block models of views.

b.   One of the outputs of the Technology Architecture is a set of assumptions.

c.   One of the outputs of the Technology Architecture is a description of the scope of the architecture.

d.   One of the outputs of the Technology Architecture is a set of conformance requirements.

e.   One of the outputs of the Technology Architecture is a set of architecture delivery and business metrics.

The Enterprise Continuum

43: The Enterprise Continuum. Indicate whether the following statements are TRUE or FALSE.

a.   The Enterprise Continuum is a virtual repository of all the architecture assets.

b.   The TRM is an example of an asset in the IT industry.

c.   The Enterprise Continuum consists of two parts: the Architecture Continuum and the Business Continuum.

d.   The Integrated Information Infrastructure Reference Model is designed to help the realization of architectures that enable and support the Boundaryless Information Flow vision.

e.   The Architecture Continuum represents a structuring of re-usable architecture assets.

The Architecture Continuum

44: The Architecture Continuum. Indicate whether the following statements are TRUE or FALSE.

a.   The Architecture Continuum ranges from Foundation Architectures, through Common Systems Architectures and industry-specific architectures, to an enterprise's own individual architectures.

b.   An example of a Foundation Architecture is a Security Architecture.

c.   An example of a Common Systems Architecture is a Management Architecture.

d.   The Technical Reference Model (TRM) and Standards Information Base (SIB) form a Foundation Architecture for The Open Group.

e.   An example of a Common Systems Architecture is a Network Architecture.

45: The Architecture Continuum continued. Indicate whether the following statements are TRUE or FALSE.
   a. A typical example of an industry-specific component is the POSC data model.
   b. Industry Architectures usually reflect requirements and standards specific to a vertical industry.
   c. Industry Architectures usually provide guidelines for testing collections of systems.
   d. Enterprise architectures are not relevant to the IT customer community.
   e. The enterprise architecture guides the final customization of the solution.

46: The Architecture Continuum continued. Indicate whether the following statements are TRUE or FALSE.
   a. A populated Solutions Continuum can be regarded as a solutions inventory or re-use library.
   b. The solution types within the Solutions Continuum are products and services, systems solutions, industry solutions, and enterprise solutions.
   c. Products are the fundamental providers of capabilities.
   d. An example of an industry solution is a security system product.
   e. Computer systems vendors are the primary provider of systems solutions.

47: The Architecture Continuum continued. Indicate whether the following statements are TRUE or FALSE.
   a. An industry solution is an implementation of an Industry Architecture which provides re-usable packages of common components and services specific to an industry.
   b. An example of an industry solution is a physical database schema.
   c. An industry solution may include not only an implementation of the Industry Architecture but also other solution elements, such as specific products.
   d. An enterprise solution is an implementation of the enterprise architecture that provides the required business functions.
   e. The Enterprise Continuum should be interpreted as representing strictly chained relationships.

Foundation Architecture: Technical Reference Model

48: The Foundation Architecture. Indicate whether the following statements are TRUE or FALSE.

a. The Technical Reference Model (TRM) provides a model and taxonomy of generic platform services.

b. The Standards Information Base (SIB) provides a database of standards that can be used to define services and other components.

c. The TRM is universally applicable and can be used to build any system architecture.

d. The list of standards and specifications in the SIB concentrates on technology-specific standards.

e. Any TRM has two main components: a taxonomy, which defines terminology, and an associated TRM graphic.

49: The Foundation Architecture continued. Indicate whether the following statements are TRUE or FALSE.

a. It is easy when developing an architecture framework to choose a TRM that works for everyone.

b. The TOGAF TRM was originally derived from the Technical Architecture Framework for Information Management (TAFIM) TRM.

c. The TOGAF TRM aims to emphasize interoperability as well as portability.

d. The objective of the TRM is to enable structured definition of the standardized Application Platform and its associated interfaces.

e. Other architecture models are not recommended for use with TOGAF.

50: The Foundation Architecture continued. Indicate whether the following statements are TRUE or FALSE.

a. The TRM has three parts (Application Software, Application Platform, and Communications Infrastructure) connected by two interfaces (Application Platform Interface and Communications Infrastructure Interface).

b. The high-level TRM seeks to maximize Portability and Interoperability.

c. The high-level model seeks to reflect the increasingly important role of the Internet as the basis for inter- and intra-enterprise interoperability.

d. The horizontal dimension of the high-level model represents diversity.

e. The shape of the model is intended to emphasize the importance of maximum diversity at the interface between the Application Platform and the Communications Infrastructure.

51: The TRM in Detail. Indicate whether the following statements are TRUE or FALSE.

    a.   All IT architectures derived from TOGAF should be very similar.

    b.   The detailed TRM recognizes two categories of Application Software: Business and Infrastructure.

    c.   An example of a business application is a set of patient record management services used in the Medical industry.

    d.   An example of a business application is a set of electronic mail client services.

    e.   An example of an infrastructure application is a set of calendar and scheduling services.

52: The TRM in Detail. Indicate whether the following statements are TRUE or FALSE.

    a.   The Application Platform in the TOGAF TRM is a single, generic, conceptual entity.

    b.   In the TOGAF TRM, the Application Platform contains all possible services.

    c.   Service bundles are represented in a Technology Architecture in the form of building blocks.

    d.   The IT architect must define the set of optimal Solution Building Blocks (SBBs).

    e.   The set of services identified and defined for the Application Platform is likely to stay the same over time.

53: The TRM in Detail continued. Indicate whether the following statements are TRUE or FALSE.

    a.   Services in the Application Platform may support each other.

    b.   A key goal of architecture development is for service modules to be replaceable.

    c.   Use of private interfaces among service modules facilitates substitution.

    d.   Private interfaces represent a risk that should be highlighted to facilitate future transition.

    e.   The TRM may be extended with new service categories as new technology appears.

54: The TRM in Detail continued. Indicate whether the following statements are TRUE or FALSE.

    a.   The Communications Infrastructure provides the basic services to interconnect systems.

b. The Communications Infrastructure provides the basic mechanisms for opaque transfer of data.

c. The Communications Infrastructure is concerned with switches, service providers, and the physical transmission media.

d. The Internet is rarely used as the basis of a Communications Infrastructure for enterprise integration.

e. There is a steady increase in the range of applications linking to the network for distributed operation.

55: The TRM in Detail continued (the API). Indicate whether the following statements are TRUE or FALSE.

a. The interface between the Application Software and the underlying Application Platform is called the Application Platform Interface (API).

b. For portability, the API definition must include the syntax and semantics of just the programmatic interface.

c. Portability depends on the symmetry of conformance of both applications and the platform to the architected API.

d. An application may use several APIs.

e. An application may use different APIs for different implementations of the same service.

56: The TRM in Detail continued (qualities). Indicate whether the following statements are TRUE or FALSE.

a. For management services to be effective manageability must be a pervasive quality of all platform services, applications, and Communications Infrastructure services.

b. System-wide implementation of security requires not only a set of security services but also the support of software in other parts of the TRM.

c. Qualities are specified in detail during the development of a Target Architecture.

d. The four main service qualities presently identified in the TRM taxonomy are Availability, Assurance, Usability, and Adaptability.

e. The best way of making sure that qualities are not forgotten is to perform a gap analysis.

Foundation Architecture: Standards Information Base

57: The SIB is a database of facts and guidance about information systems standards. Indicate whether the following statements are TRUE or FALSE.

    a. The SIB has three main uses: Architecture Development, Acquisition/ Procurement, and General Information.

    b. The SIB can be used to dynamically generate lists of the standards endorsed by The Open Group for use in open systems architectures.

    c. The Open Group adds value to individual standards by integrating them into sets known as Product Standards.

    d. The Open Group Product Standards are supported by a unique brand called the Open Brand.

    e. Once a Program Group has recommended a standard, it is automatically included in the SIB.

Architecture Contracts

58: Architecture Contracts. Indicate whether the following statements are TRUE or FALSE.

    a. Architecture Contracts are joint agreements between development partners and sponsors on deliverables, quality, and fitness-for-purpose of an architecture.

    b. Successful implementation of Architecture Contracts is delivered through effective architecture governance.

    c. Architecture Contracts may occur at various stages of the Architecture Development Method.

    d. The ultimate goal is a static enterprise architecture.

    e. There are three main types of Architecture Contract.

Architecture Governance

59: The nature and levels of governance. Indicate whether the following statements are TRUE or FALSE.

    a. Architecture governance is the practice and orientation by which enterprise architectures and other architectures are managed and controlled at an enterprise-wide level.

    b. Corporate governance is a broad topic and is beyond the scope of TOGAF.

    c. Governance is essentially about ensuring that business is conducted properly.

d. The CORBA framework is an open standard for control over IT.
e. Phase G of the TOGAF ADM is dedicated to implementation governance.

Architecture Principles

60: Architecture Principles. Indicate whether the following statements are TRUE or FALSE.
  a. Principles are general rules and guidelines that inform and support the way in which an organization sets about fulfilling its mission.
  b. Principles may be established at any or all of three levels: Enterprise, Information Technology, and Architecture.
  c. A good set of principles should be Understandable, Robust, Complete, Consistent, and Stable.
  d. The principle of Data Security implies that security needs must be identified and developed at the application level.
  e. The principle of Technology Independence implies the use of standards which support portability.

Building Blocks

61: Building Blocks. Indicate whether the following statements are TRUE or FALSE.
  a. A building block is a package of functionality defined to meet the business needs across an organization.
  b. A building block may interoperate with other, inter-dependent building blocks.
  c. Architecture Building Blocks define what functionality will be implemented.
  d. SBBs fulfill business requirements.
  e. Solution Building Blocks (SBBs) must be procured rather than developed.

Other Architectures and Frameworks

62: TOGAF is one of a number of architectures and architecture frameworks in use today. C4ISR is a framework developed by the US Department of Defense. Indicate whether the following statements are TRUE or FALSE.
  a. The acronym C4ISR stands for Command, Control, Computers, Communications (C4), Intelligence, Surveillance, and Reconnaissance (ISR).

    b. There is a lot of guidance in the C4ISR Architecture Framework concerning the process of describing an architecture.

    c. C4ISR is used in order to ensure interoperable and cost-effective military systems.

    d. C4ISR was a successor to the Technical Architecture Framework for Information Management (TAFIM) and has been replaced by DODAF.

    e. The sequence in which the products are built depends on the purpose of the architecture description.

63: CORBA. Indicate whether the following statements are TRUE or FALSE.

    a. CORBA is an object-oriented Applications Architecture centered on the concept of an Object Request Broker (ORB).

    b. The ORB acts as a switching center.

    c. The OMA is an application-level architecture which focuses exclusively on issues affecting distributed object-oriented systems.

    d. CORBA services are a high-level set of common object services.

    e. CORBA is not consistent with TOGAF.

64: Enterprise Architecture Planning (EAP). Indicate whether the following statements are TRUE or FALSE.

    a. EAP is a set of methods for planning the development of Information, Applications, and Technology Architectures.

    b. The EAP methodology positions four types of architecture in the sequence: Business, Data, Applications, and Technology.

    c. EAP has a Foundation Architecture.

    d. EAP does not have a taxonomy of viewpoints and views.

    e. EAP has a Standards Information Base.

65: Federal Enterprise Architecture: Practical Guide. Indicate whether the following statements are TRUE or FALSE.

    a. The purpose of this guide is to provide guidance to US federal agencies.

    b. This guide offers an end-to-end process to initiate, implement, and sustain an enterprise architecture program.

    c. This guide focuses on enterprise architecture processes, products, and roles and responsibilities.

    d. The guide addresses how enterprise architecture processes fit within an overall enterprise lifecycle.

    e. The Practical Guide's enterprise architecture processes do not align closely with the lifecycle phases of the TOGAF ADM.

66: RM-ODP. Indicate whether the following statements are TRUE or FALSE.
   a. RM-ODP provides a framework to support the development of standards for distributed processing in heterogeneous environments.
   b. RM-ODP uses an object modeling approach.
   c. RM-ODP has five viewpoints.
   d. TOGAF coverage is a subset of that provided by RM-ODP.
   e. The solution-level building blocks of TOGAF map to the Technology and Engineering viewpoints of RM-ODP.

67: TAFIM. Indicate whether the following statements are TRUE or FALSE.
   a. The US Department of Defense Technical Architecture Framework for Information Management (TAFIM) was used as the basis of TOGAF Version 1.
   b. TAFIM was developed from the Guide to the POSIX Open System Environment.
   c. TAFIM and TOGAF have very little in common.
   d. The TOGAF Architecture Development Method (ADM) was originally based on parts of TAFIM.
   e. TAFIM has been superseded by C4ISR Architecture Framework (1999), JTA (1997), and the DoD 1999 Technical Reference Model (TRM).

68: The Zachman Framework. Indicate whether the following statements are TRUE or FALSE.
   a. The Zachman Framework is a framework providing a view of the subjects and models needed to develop a complete enterprise architecture.
   b. Zachman based his framework on practices in traditional architecture and engineering.
   c. The viewpoints that TOGAF recommends are all included in the Zachman Framework.
   d. The Zachman Framework provides a very comprehensive and well-established taxonomy of the various viewpoints, models, and other artifacts.
   e. The Zachman Framework says nothing about the processes for developing viewpoints or conformant views.

Appendix C

Test Yourself Examination Paper Answers

C.1 Answers to the Examination Paper

This appendix contains a table of the answers to the Examination Paper in Appendix B.

Question Number	a	b	c	d	e	# Correct	Score
1	F	F	T	T	T		
2	T	T	T	F	T		
3	T	F	T	T	F		
4	T	T	F	T	F		
5	T	F	T	F	T		
6	T	T	F	T	F		
7	T	F	T	T	F		
8	T	F	T	T	F		
9	F	F	T	T	F		
10	T	T	F	F	T		
11	T	T	F	T	F		
12	T	T	F	T	F		
13	F	F	T	T	F		
14	T	T	F	F	F		
15	T	T	F	F	T		
16	F	T	T	F	T		
17	T	T	F	T	T		
18	T	T	F	T	F		
19	T	T	F	F	T		
20	F	T	T	F	F		
21	T	F	T	F	F		
22	T	F	T	F	F		
23	F	T	T	F	F		
24	T	F	F	T	T		
25	T	T	F	F	F		

Question Number	a	b	c	d	e	# Correct	Score
26	F	F	T	T	F		
27	T	T	T	F	F		
28	F	T	F	T	F		
29	F	F	F	T	T		
30	T	T	F	F	F		
31	F	T	T	F	F		
32	F	T	F	T	T		
33	F	T	T	T	F		
34	T	T	F	F	F		
35	T	T	F	T	F		
36	T	F	F	T	F		
37	T	T	T	F	F		
38	F	F	T	T	F		
39	T	T	T	F	F		
40	T	T	F	F	F		
41	T	T	F	F	T		
42	T	T	F	F	F		
43	T	T	F	T	T		
44	T	F	T	T	T		
45	T	T	T	F	T		
46	T	T	T	F	T		
47	T	T	T	T	F		
48	T	T	T	F	T		
49	F	T	T	T	F		
50	T	T	T	T	F		
51	F	T	T	F	T		
52	T	T	T	T	F		
53	T	T	F	T	T		
54	T	T	T	F	T		
55	T	F	T	T	T		
56	T	T	T	T	F		
57	T	T	T	T	F		
58	T	T	T	F	T		
59	T	T	T	F	T		
60	T	T	T	F	T		
61	T	T	T	T	F		

Question Number	a	b	c	d	e	# Correct	Score
62	T	F	T	T	T		
63	T	T	T	F	F		
64	T	T	F	T	F		
65	T	T	T	T	F		
66	T	T	T	F	T		
67	T	T	F	T	T		
68	T	T	F	T	T		

C.2 Scoring the Examination

For each question, calculate the number of parts answered correctly and enter that in the # Correct column.

If you answer five parts (a,b,c,d,e) correctly for a question, then you score 3 points. If you answer four parts correctly, then you score 1 point. If you answer three parts correctly, then you score half a point. If you answer two or fewer parts correctly, then you score zero points for that question.

The target score for this examination is 104 points or more.

TOGAF 8 Certified Course Syllabus

D.1 Course Syllabus Mapping

This appendix provides a mapping between the TOGAF 8 Certified Course Syllabus and the sections in this Study Guide.

There are six Topic Areas in the syllabus:

- TOGAF 8 Architecture Development Method (ADM) – Process
- TOGAF 8 Architecture Development Method (ADM) – Information Sets
- TOGAF Foundation Architecture
- The Enterprise Continuum
- TOGAF and Other Architectures/Frameworks
- Architecture Governance

1: TOGAF 8 Architecture Development Method (ADM) – Process

Preliminary Phase: Framework and Principles

Topic		Syllabus Reference(s)
1.P.1	Defining "How we do Architecture"	4.4.1
1.P.2	Defining the Framework to be used	4.4.1.2
1.P.3	Defining Architecture Principles	4.4.1.1
1.P.4	Establishing IT Architecture Governance	4.4.2

Phase A: Architecture Vision

Topic		Syllabus Reference(s)
1.A.1	Project Establishment	5.4.1
1.A.2	Identifying Business Principles, Business Goals, and Business Drivers	5.4.2
1.A.3	Reviewing Architecture Principles	5.4.3
1.A.4	Defining Scope	5.4.4
1.A.5	Defining Constraints	5.4.5
1.A.6	Defining Stakeholders and Concerns, Business Requirements, and Architecture Vision	5.4.6

| 1.A.7 | Documenting Statement of Architecture Work and Gaining Approval | 5.4.7 |

Phase B: Business Architecture

Topic		Syllabus Reference(s)
1.B.1	Developing a Business Baseline Description	6.5.1
1.B.2	Reference Models, Viewpoints, and Tools	6.5.2
1.B.3	Create Business Architecture Model(s)	6.5.3
1.B.4	Select Business Architecture Building Blocks	6.5.4
1.B.5	Conduct Checkpoint Review of Architecture Model	6.5.5
1.B.6	Review Non-functional (Qualitative) Criteria	6.5.6
1.B.7	Complete the Business Architecture	6.5.7
1.B.8	Gap Analysis and Report	6.5.8

Phase C: Information Systems Architecture – Data

Topic		Syllabus Reference(s)
1.CD.1	Developing a Data Baseline Description	8.4.1
1.CD.2	Principles, Reference Models, Viewpoints, and Tools	8.4.2
1.CD.3	Create Data Architecture Model(s)	8.4.3
1.CD.4	Select Data Architecture Building Blocks	8.4.4
1.CD.5	Conduct checkpoint review of architecture model	8.4.5
1.CD.6	Review non-functional (qualitative) criteria	8.4.6
1.CD.7	Complete the Data Architecture	8.4.7
1.CD.8	Gap analysis and report	8.4.9

Phase C: Information Systems Architecture – Applications

Topic		Syllabus Reference(s)
1.CA.1	Developing an Applications Baseline Description	9.4.1
1.CA.2	Principles, Reference Models, Viewpoints, and Tools	9.4.2
1.CA.3	Create Applications Architecture Model(s)	9.4.3
1.CA.4	Select Applications Architecture Building Blocks	9.4.4
1.CA.5	Conduct checkpoint review of architecture model	9.4.5
1.CA.6	Review non-functional (qualitative) criteria	9.4.6
1.CA.7	Complete the Applications Architecture	9.4.7
1.CA.8	Gap analysis and report	9.4.8

Phase D: Technology Architecture

Topic		Syllabus Reference(s)
1.D.1	Create Technology Baseline Description	10.4.1
1.D.2	Create Target Technology Architecture	10.4.2
1.D.2.1	Create a Baseline Description in the TOGAF format	10.5.1
1.D.2.2	Consider different architecture viewpoints	10.5.2
1.D.2.3	Create an architecture model of building blocks	10.5.3
1.D.2.4	Select the services portfolio required per building block	10.5.4
1.D.2.5	Confirm that business goals and objectives are met	10.5.5
1.D.2.6	Determine criteria for specification selection	10.5.6
1.D.2.7	Complete the architecture definition	10.5.7
1.D.2.8	Conduct gap analysis	10.5.8

Phase E: Opportunities and Solutions

Topic		Syllabus Reference(s)
1.E.1	Identify key business drivers constraining sequence of implementation	11.5.1
1.E.2	Review gap analysis	11.5.2
1.E.3	Brainstorm technical requirements from functional perspective	11.5.3
1.E.4	Brainstorm co-existence and interoperability requirements	11.5.4
1.E.5	Architecture assessment and gap analysis	11.5.5
1.E.6	Identify major work packages or projects, classify as new development, purchase opportunity, or re-use of existing system	11.5.6

Phase F: Migration Planning

Topic		Syllabus Reference(s)
1.F.1	Prioritize projects	12.5.1
1.F.2	Estimate resource requirements and availability	12.5.2
1.F.3	Perform cost/benefit assessment of the various migration projects	12.5.3
1.F.4	Perform risk assessment	12.5.4
1.F.5	Generate implementation roadmap (time-lined)	12.5.5
1.F.6	Document Migration Plan	12.5.6

Phase G: Implementation Governance

Topic		Syllabus Reference(s)
1.G.1	Formulate project recommendations	13.5.1
1.G.2	Document Architecture Contract	13.5.2
1.G.3	Ongoing Implementation Governance and Architecture Compliance Review	13.5.3

Phase H: Architecture Change Management

Topic		Syllabus Reference(s)
1.H.1	Ongoing monitoring of technology changes	14.5.1
1.H.2	Ongoing monitoring of business changes	14.5.2

| 1.H.3 | Assessment of changes and development of position to act | 14.5.3 |
| 1.H.4 | Meeting of Architecture Board (or other governing council) to decide on handling changes (technology and business) | 14.5.4 |

Requirements Management

Topic		Syllabus Reference(s)
1.R.1	Key steps in the Requirements Management process	3.9, 3.9.2

2: TOGAF 8 Architecture Development Method (ADM) – Information Sets

Topic		Syllabus Reference(s)
2.1	Framework Definition	2.2.4, 2.2.5, 2.2.7, Chapter 3, 15.2.1
2.2	Architecture Principles	4.4.1.1, 15.2.2
2.3	Business Principles, Goals, and Drivers	15.2.3
2.4	IT Governance Strategy	15.2.4
2.5	Request for Architecture Work	15.2.5
2.6	Statement of Architecture Work	15.2.6
2.7	Architecture Vision	15.2.7
2.8	Business Architecture	15.2.8
2.9	Business Architecture Report	15.2.9
2.10	Business Requirements	15.2.10
2.11	Technical Requirements	15.2.11
2.12	Gap Analysis	15.2.12
2.13	Data Architecture	15.2.13
2.14	Data Architecture Report	15.2.14
2.15	Applications Architecture	15.2.15
2.16	Applications Architecture Report	15.2.16
2.17	Technology Architecture	15.2.17
2.18	Technology Architecture Report	15.2.18
2.19	Architecture Viewpoints	15.2.19
2.20	Architecture Views	15.2.20
2.21	Re-usable Architecture Building Blocks	15.2.21
2.22	Re-usable Solution Building Blocks	15.2.22

| 4.1.4 | The relationship to the Solutions Continuum | 19.5 |

4.2: Solutions Continuum

Topic		Syllabus Reference(s)
4.2.1	The concept of the Solutions Continuum	20.2
4.2.2	Moving around the Solutions Continuum	20.3
4.2.3	The Solutions Continuum as a repository of re-usable Solution Building Blocks	20.4

5: TOGAF and Other Architectures/Frameworks

5.1: The Positioning of TOGAF

Topic		Syllabus Reference(s)
5.1.1	Positioning information	21.2
5.1.2	Explaining it to users	21.2

5.2: Examples

Topic	Syllabus Reference(s)
Examples of other Architecture Frameworks referenced in TOGAF (for example, C4ISR, Enterprise Architecture Planning, Zachman Framework, etc.)	21.3

6: Architecture Governance

6.1: Introduction to Governance

Topic		Syllabus Reference(s)
6.1.1	Nature of Governance	22.2.1
6.1.2	Levels of Governance	22.2.2

6.2: TOGAF Architecture Governance Framework

Topic		Syllabus Reference(s)
6.2.1	Conceptual Structure	**22.3.1**
6.2.2	Organizational Structure	22.3.2

6.3: Architecture Governance in Practice

Topic	Syllabus Reference(s)
6.3.1 Architecture Board	22.4.2
6.3.2 Architecture Compliance	22.4.3
6.3.3 Architecture Contracts	22.4.4

Glossary

ADM Architecture Development Method

Architecture Framework
A tool for assisting in the production of architectures. An architecture
framework consists of a Technical Reference Model, a method for
architecture development, and a list of component standards, specifications,
products, and their inter-relationships that can be used to build up
architectures.

Architecture
Architecture has two meanings depending upon its contextual usage:
1. A formal description of a system, or a detailed plan of the system at
   component level to guide its implementation
2. The structure of components, their inter-relationships, and the principles
   and guidelines governing their design and evolution over time

Architecture Continuum
A part of the Enterprise Continuum. The Architecture Continuum provides a
repository of architecture elements with increasing detail and specialization.
This Continuum begins with foundational definitions like reference models,
core strategies, and basic building blocks. From there it spans to Industry
Architectures and all the way to an organization's specific architecture.

Enterprise
The highest level in an organization; includes all missions and functions.

Enterprise Continuum
Comprises two complementary concepts: the Architecture Continuum and
the Solutions Continuum. Together these are a range of definitions with
increasing specificity, from foundational definitions and agreed enterprise
strategies all the way to architectures and implementations in specific
organizations. Such coexistence of abstraction and concreteness in an

enterprise can be a real source of confusion. The Enterprise Continuum also doubles as a powerful tool to turn confusion and resulting conflicts into progress.

Information System
The computer-based portion of a business system.

Repository
A system that manages all of the data of an enterprise, including data and process models and other enterprise information. Hence, the data in a repository is much more extensive than that in a data dictionary, which generally defines only the data making up a database.

Solutions Continuum
A part of the Enterprise Continuum. The Solutions Continuum contains implementations of the corresponding definitions in the Architecture Continuum. In this way it becomes a repository of re-usable solutions for future implementation efforts.

Technical Reference Model
A structure which allows the components of an information system to be described in a consistent manner.

Time Horizon
The timeframe over which the potential impact is to be measured.

TRM   Technical Reference Model

View
A representation of a whole system from the perspective of a related set of concerns.

Viewpoint
A specification of the conventions for constructing and using a view. A viewpoint acts as a pattern or template of the view, from which to develop individual views. A viewpoint establishes the purposes and audience for a view, the ways in which the view is documented (e.g., for visual modeling), and the ways in which it is used (e.g., for analysis)

Index